Accession no.
36184663

WITHDRAWN

Thomas'
Sentencing
Referencer
2015

by David Thomas
Q.C., LL.D.

edited by Lyndon Harris
LL.B. (Hons), LL.M.

LIS - LIBRARY

Date	Fund
29-4-15	lw-che

Order No.
2597068·

University of Chester

SWEET & MAXWELL  **THOMSON REUTERS**

Published in 2015 by Sweet & Maxwell, Friars House, 160 Blackfriars Road,
London SE1 8EZ
part of Thomson Reuters (Professional) UK Limited
(Registered in England & Wales, Company No 1679046.
Registered Office and address for service:
Aldgate House, 33 Aldgate High Street, London EC3N 1DL)

Typeset by LBJ Typesetting Ltd
of Kingsclere
Printed and bound by CPI Group (UK) Ltd, Croydon, CR0 4YY

For further information on our products and services, visit
www.sweetandmaxwell.co.uk

No natural forests were destroyed to make this product; only farmed timber was
used and replanted.

A CIP catalogue record of this book is available from the British Library.

ISBN 9780414035409

© 2015 Thomson Reuters (Professional) UK Limited

Thomson Reuters and the Thomson Reuters logo are trademarks of Thomson
Reuters.

Crown copyright material is reproduced with the permission of the Controller of
HMSO and the Queen's Printer for Scotland.

All rights reserved. No part of this publication may be reproduced or transmitted
in any form or by any means, or stored in any retrieval system of any nature
without prior written permission, except for permitted fair dealing under the
Copyright, Designs and Patents Act 1988, or in accordance with the terms of a
licence issued by the Copyright Licensing Agency in respect of photocopying and/
or reprographic reproduction. Application for permission for other use of
copyright material including permission to reproduce extracts in other published
works shall be made to the publishers. Full acknowledgement of author, publisher
and source must be given.

Contents

Part 1—Sentencing Topics

Part 2—Maximum Sentences (Indictable Offences)

Part 3—Charts and Tables

Part 1:

Sentencing topics

Adjournment

MAGISTRATES' COURTS ACT 1980 s.10

References: Current Sentencing Practice L7–1; Archbold 5–15

A **magistrates' court** may adjourn after conviction to enable enquiries to be made or to determine the most suitable method of dealing with the case. The adjournment must not be for more than four weeks at a time, or three weeks if the offender is in custody.

The **Crown Court** may adjourn after conviction for similar purposes; there is no statutory limitation. The Crown Court may adjourn part of the sentence only.

(Where the court postpones hearings in connection with confiscation orders, the total period of postponement must not exceed six months or two years from the date of conviction, according to which statutory scheme applies, unless there are exceptional circumstances: see **Confiscation Orders—Postponement of Proceedings.**)

The Bail Act 1976 s.4 applies if the court adjourns for inquiries.

On adjourning, the court should avoid giving the offender any reason to expect that he will be dealt with by means of a sentence not involving custody. If the offender is given the impression that the court will deal with him without sending him to custody, it may not be open to the court which adjourns, or any other court dealing with the offender subsequently, to impose a custodial sentence.

A magistrates' court which adjourns after convicting a defendant of an either way offence should avoid giving the defendant any reason to expect that he will not be committed to the Crown Court for sentence.

Advance Indication of Sentence

R. v Goodyear [2006] 1 Cr.App.R(S.) 6 (p.23)

References: Current Sentencing Practice L1–1; Archbold 5–110

A judge may give an advance indication of the maximum sentence which would be imposed **if a plea of guilty were tendered at the stage the indication is sought**.

The judge should not give an advance indication unless one is sought by the defendant. The judge retains an unfettered discretion to refuse to give an advance indication. The judge may reserve his position until he feels able to give an advance indication of sentence, for instance where reports on the defendant are expected.

Once an advance indication of sentence is given, it is binding on the judge and any other judge who becomes responsible for the case. If the defendant does not plead guilty within a reasonable time after the advance indication has been given, the indication will cease to have effect.

The process of seeking an advance indication should be initiated by the defence; the defence advocate should have written instructions from the defendant. An indication should not be sought while there is any uncertainty about an acceptable plea or the factual basis of sentencing.

The judge should not become involved in discussions which link the acceptable plea to the sentence which is likely to be imposed. Advance indications should not be given on alternative bases.

Particular care should be taken in cases where the defendant is charged with one or more specified offences. Counsel should inform the judge that one or more of the offences is a specified offence. The judge may decline to give any indication; it he does give an indication, it may in qualified terms, depending on the outcome of the assessment of the defendant's dangerousness.

The right of the Attorney General to refer a sentence to the Court of Appeal on the ground that it is unduly lenient is not affected by the giving of an advance indication of sentence.

Hearings relating to advance indications of sentence should normally take place in open court.

Age of Offender

P.C.C.(S.)A. 2000 s.164(1)

References: Current Sentencing Practice E2–2AA; Archbold 5–11

For the purposes of liability to custodial sentences and community orders, community rehabilitation orders, community punishment orders, community punishment and rehabilitation orders, curfew orders, drug abstinence orders, drug treatment and testing orders, exclusion orders, supervision orders and attendance centre orders **the age of the offender is his age on the day of conviction**, except in the exceptional cases listed below.

For the purposes of sentences of imprisonment, detention in a young offender institution, detention under the P.C.C.(S.)A. 2000 s.91 or detention and training orders, **the age of an offender is deemed to be what it appears to the court to be**, after the court has considered any available evidence, but where it is apparent that the age of the offender is in doubt or dispute, the court should adjourn and obtain proper evidence of age before sentencing.

Exceptional cases

An offender committed to the Crown Court for sentence under the P.C.C.(S.)A. 2000 ss.3, 4 or 6, must be sentenced on the basis of his age on the day he appears before the Crown Court. *This does not apply to an offender committed for sentence under the P.C.C.(S.)A. 2000 s.3C (dangerous young offenders).*

An offender subject to a community rehabilitation order, community punishment order, community punishment and rehabilitation order, curfew order, drug abstinence order, drug treatment and testing order, or exclusion order, who is convicted by the Crown Court, or who appears before the Crown Court for sentence, while the community order is in force, must be sentenced on the basis of his age when he appears before the Crown Court if the Crown Court revokes the community order and passes a further sentence for the offence.

An offender who is found to be in breach of a community rehabilitation order, community punishment order, community punishment and rehabilitation order, curfew order, drug abstinence order, drug treatment and testing order, or exclusion order and in whose case the order is revoked must be sentenced on the basis of his age when he appears before the court which revokes the order.

An offender who is subject to a community order made under the Criminal Justice Act 2003 in whose case the community order is revoked following a breach or subsequent conviction must be sentenced on the basis of his age when the original order was made.

Where the court revokes a youth rehabilitation order and resentences the offender for the original offence, it may deal with him in any way in which the court could have dealt with the offender for that offence.

Where an offender who has been the subject of a conditional discharge is convicted of a further offence and the conditional discharge is revoked and a sentence imposed for the original offence, he must be sentenced on the basis of his age when he is sentenced.

An offender convicted at any age of a murder committed when he was under 18 must be sentenced to be detained during Her Majesty's Pleasure.

The power to make a disqualification order depends on the offender's age when he committed the offence.

The obligation to impose a required minimum sentence under the Firearms Act 1968 s.51A depends on the offender's age when the offence was committed.

Aggravated Drug Trafficking

MISUSE OF DRUGS ACT 1971 s.4A

References: Current Sentencing Practice A19–1A; Archbold 27–28a

If an offender over 18 is convicted of an offence of supplying or offering to supply a controlled drug, and either the offence was committed in the vicinity of a school at any time when the premises were in use, or one hour before or after such time, or the offender used a courier who was under the age of 18, the court must treat that fact as an aggravating factor and must state in open court that the offence was so aggravated.

This provision applies to offences committed on or after January 1, 2006.

Alteration of Sentence

P.C.C.(S.)A. 2000 s.155; MAGISTRATES' COURTS ACT 1980 s.142

References: Current Sentencing Practice L10–1; Archbold 5–1289

The Crown Court may vary or rescind a sentence which it has imposed or an order which it has made, **within specified time limits**. *The Crown Court must be constituted as it was when the original sentence was imposed or order was made*, except that if the court included one or more justices of the peace, one or all of them may be omitted.

The power may not be exercised in relation to any sentence or order if an appeal, or an application for leave to appeal, against that sentence or order has been determined.

A magistrates' court may vary or rescind a sentence or order at any time after the sentence has been passed or the order made, unless the Crown Court or the High Court has determined an appeal against the sentence or the conviction on which it is based. *There is no time limit for magistrates' courts.*

The time limit for the Crown Court is **56 days beginning with the day on which the sentence was imposed or the order was made**. Where orders have been made on different dates in respect of the same conviction the period of 56 days begins to run on the day on which the particular order which it is proposed to vary was made.

The relevant time limit must be strictly observed, but where a sentence has been passed or order made which is defective in form, it may be permissible to correct the error after the expiration of the relevant time limit, so long as the correction can be treated as a matter of form rather than substance.

If the Crown Court rescinds a sentence within the permitted period for variation or rescission, without imposing a further sentence, it may adjourn sentence for such period as may be appropriate, without regard to the time limit.

There is no restriction on the nature of the variation in sentence which may be made. In appropriate circumstances the court may substitute a sentence or order which is more severe than the sentence originally passed. The power is not limited to the correction of slips of the tongue or minor errors made when sentence was originally passed.

It is permissible to correct a sentence which is unlawful in the form in which it has been passed.

Where the court has been persuaded to pass a particular form of sentence, or a sentence of a particular length, on the basis of the existence of specific mitigating factors, the court may review the sentence and substitute a more severe sentence if it subsequently appears that the court has been misled and that the mitigating factors did not exist. Such a decision should not be made without proper inquiry and giving the offender an opportunity to dispute the allegation that he has deceived the court.

It is wrong for a sentencer to increase a sentence simply because on reflection he considers that the sentence he has passed was too lenient. There is no objection to reducing a sentence because on second thoughts it appears to have been too severe.

It is wrong to vary a sentence which has been passed on the ground that the offender has reacted to the sentence by misbehaving in the dock and addressing abusive comments to the judge or other persons present.

It is not clear whether a sentence which has been varied once can be varied a second time.

As a general rule, the power to vary a sentence should be exercised only in open court and in the presence of the offender after hearing his counsel, who should be advised of the nature of the alteration which the court proposes to make.

Where the Crown Court passes part of a sentence and expressly postpones passing some other part of the sentence, the time limits do not apply.

Antecedents Statements

See *CPD Preliminary Proceedings 10A* [2013] EWCA Crim 1631; *Archbold* 5–72.

Anti-Social Behaviour Order on Conviction

CRIME AND DISORDER ACT 1998 s.1C

References: Current Sentencing Practice H10–1A; Archbold 5–1198

A court dealing with an offender for any offence committed on or after December 2, 2002, may make an order if it considers that the offender has acted, at any time since April 1, 1999, in a manner that *caused or was likely to cause harassment, alarm or distress to one or more persons not of the same household as himself and that an order is necessary to protect persons in any place in England and Wales from further anti-social acts by him.*

The order may prohibit the offender from doing anything described in the order.

The test for making an order under s.1C is one *of necessity to protect the public from further anti-social acts by the offender.*

The terms of the order must be precise and capable of being understood by the offender.

The findings of fact giving rise to the making of the order must be recorded.

The order must be explained to the offender.

The exact terms of the order must be pronounced in open court and the written order must accurately reflect the order as pronounced.

The order may be for a specified period (not less than two years) or indefinite.

The court may make an order if the prosecutor asks it to do so, or if the court thinks it is appropriate to do so.

For the purpose of deciding whether to make an order under this section the court may consider evidence led by the prosecution and the defence, whether or not the evidence would have been admissible in the proceedings in which the offender was convicted.

An order should not be made simply for the purpose of subjecting the offender to an increased maximum sentence for conduct which would otherwise be a summary offence.

An order may be made only in addition to a sentence imposed for the offence, or a conditional discharge.

An order may be suspended during any period when the offender is detained in legal custody.

An offender subject to an order, the DPP or the relevant authority, may apply to the court which made the order for it to be varied or discharged. An order may not be varied or discharged within two years on the application of the offender unless the DPP consents. An order may not be varied or discharged within two years on the application of the DPP or the relevant authority unless the offender consents.

If an offender is convicted of a breach of an antisocial behaviour order as a result of conduct which would amount to the commission of a distinct criminal offence, the sentence for the breach of the order is not limited to the maximum sentence which would be available for the criminal offence.

A court which makes an order under s.1C in respect of a person under 18 years of age must make **an individual support order** if the court considers that the "individual support conditions" are satisfied. The "individual support conditions" are that an individual support order would be desirable in the interests of preventing any repetition of the kind of behaviour which led to the making of the anti-social behaviour order, or of any order varying that order, where the order has been varied as a result of further anti-social behaviour by the defendant. An individual support order may not be made if the defendant is already subject to an individual support order. **An individual support order may be made only if the court has been notified by the Secretary of State that arrangements for implementing individual support orders are available in the area in which the defendant resides or will reside.**

If the court is not satisfied that the individual support conditions are fulfilled, it must state in open court that it is not so satisfied and why it is not.

The individual support order may contain those requirements that the court considers desirable in the interests of preventing any repetition of the kind of behaviour which led to the making of the order. They may include requirements that the offender should participate in activities specified in the order, present himself to a person or persons specified in the order, or comply with any arrangements relating to education. The requirements or directions given under an individual support order may not require the defendant to attend on more than two days in any week. Requirements must avoid any conflict with the defendant's religious beliefs and any interference with his normal work or education.

Before making an individual support order, the court must obtain from a social worker or a member of a youth offending team any information which it considers necessary in order to determine whether the conditions for making an order are fulfilled, and what requirements should be imposed by the order. *The court must explain to the defendant in ordinary language the effect of the order the requirements proposed to be included in it, the consequences which may follow if he fails to comply with any of those requirements; and that the court has power to review the order on the application either of the defendant or of the responsible officer.*

If an order under s.1C is made in respect of a person under the age of 17, the order may specify a relevant authority as being responsible for carrying out a review of the operation of the order.

Repeal

The provisions relating to imposing an ASBO on conviction were repealed by the Anti-social Behaviour, Crime and Policing Act 2014, with effect from October 20, 2014. The repeal applies to proceedings commenced on or after that date. For proceedings commenced before that date, an ASBO remains available.

Existing ASBOs remain in force and may be varied or discharged, but the length of the order cannot be extended. Any ASBO still in force five years after October 20, 2014 continues in force as if the provisions of the order were provisions of a criminal behaviour order.

Breach proceedings are unaffected.

Assistance to Prosecutor

SERIOUS ORGANISED CRIME AND POLICE ACT 2005 s.73

References: Current Sentencing Practice A20–1; Archbold 5–132

If a defendant who has **pleaded guilty** in proceedings in the Crown Court, or who has been committed to the Crown Court for sentence following a plea of guilty, has entered a **written agreement** with a specified prosecutor, to assist or offer to assist the investigator or prosecutor in relation to the offence to which he has pleaded guilty *or any other offence*, the court may take into account the extent and nature of the assistance given or offered in determining what sentence to pass.

The extent to which the assistance given or offered may affect the sentence is a matter within the discretion of the sentencing court.

If the court passes a sentence which is less than it would otherwise have passed, the court must **state in open court that it has passed a lesser sentence than it would otherwise have passed, and what the greater sentence would have been**. *This obligation does not apply if the court thinks that it would not be in the public interest to disclose that the sentence has been discounted.* Where no statement is made in open court, the court must give written notice of the fact that it has passed a lesser sentence, and what the greater sentence would have been, to the prosecutor and to the defendant.

Nothing in any enactment which requires that a "minimum sentence" is passed in respect of any offence or an offence of any description or by reference to the circumstances of any offender affects the power of a court to take into account the extent and nature of this assistance given or offered.

In a case of **murder**, nothing in any enactment which requires the court to take into account "certain matters" for the purposes of making an order which determines or has the effect of determining the minimum period of imprisonment which the offender must serve affects the power of the court to take into account the extent and nature of the assistance given or offered.

Where the defendant has been sentenced in the Crown Court, and has received a discounted sentence as a consequence of having made a written agreement to give assistance to the prosecutor or investigator of an offence, but has *knowingly failed "to any extent" to give assistance in accordance with the agreement*, a specified prosecutor may refer the case back to the court if the person concerned is still serving his sentence, and the prosecutor thinks that it is in the interest of justice to do so. The case so referred must if possible be heard by the judge who passed the original sentence. If the court is "satisfied" that a person whose sentence has been discounted has "knowingly failed to give the assistance", it may substitute for the sentence which has been referred "such greater sentence" as it thinks appropriate, provided that the new sentence does not exceed the sentence which it would have passed if the agreement had not been made.

Where the defendant has received a discounted sentence in consequence of having entered a written agreement to give assistance, and having given the assistance in accordance with the original agreement makes a further written agreement to give further assistance, the defendant's sentence may be referred to the Crown Court.

Where the defendant has received a sentence which is not discounted, but in pursuance of a written agreement made subsequently to the imposition of sentence, gives or offers to give assistance to the prosecutor or investigator, the defendant's sentence may be referred to the Crown Court, whether or not he pleaded guilty to the offence (except where he was convicted of murder following a trial).

On such a reference, the court may take into account the extent and nature of the assistance given or offered, and substitute for the original sentence "such lesser sentence as it thinks appropriate".

Where an offender who has pleaded guilty to murder offers or gives assistance after sentence, his case may be referred if the prosecutor chooses to do so.

On the hearing of a reference, or any other proceedings arising in consequence of a reference, the court may exclude from the proceedings anyone other than an officer of the court, a party to the proceedings or legal representatives of the parties, and may give such directions as it thinks appropriate prohibiting the publication of any matter relating to the proceedings, including the fact that the reference has been made. Such an order may be made only to the extent that it is necessary to do so to protect the safety of any person, and is in the interests of justice.

The statutory provisions do not replace the conventional practice by which a defendant who is unable or unwilling to enter onto a written agreement may ask the prosecuting or investigating body to produce a "text" setting out the details of the assistance or information provided by the defendant.

Attendance Centre Order

P.C.C.(S.)A. 2000 s.60

References: Current Sentencing Practice E7–1A

General

This order used to be available upon conviction, but following a statutory repeal (effective from November 30, 2009) it is now available only in limited circumstances.

Making the order

Availability: Where a court would have power, but for section 89 below (restrictions on imprisonment of young offenders and defaulters), to commit a person aged under 21 to prison in default of payment of any sum of money or for failing to do or abstain from doing anything required to be done or left undone, or a court has power to commit a person aged at least 21 but under 25 to prison in default of payment of any sum of money, the court may, if it has been notified by the Secretary of State that an attendance centre is available for the reception of persons of his description, order him to attend at such a centre, to be specified in the order, for such number of hours as may be so specified: PCC(S)A 2000 s.60(1).

Additionally, those in contempt of court where it appears to the court they are aged 17 or over may be made subject to an attendance centre order: CCA 1981 s.14(2A).

The order: The court may order the individual to attend at such a centre, to be specified in the order, for such number of hours as may be so specified: PCC(S)A 2000 s.60(1).

Setting the number of hours

Under 14: An attendance centre order is normally for 12 hours. The court may specify less than 12 hours if the offender is under the age of 14 and the court considers that 12 hours would be excessive, having regard to his age and any other circumstances: PCC(S)A 2000 s.60(3).

Under 16: The court may specify more than 12 hours if the court considers that 12 hours would be inadequate. If the offender is under 16 the maximum number of hours is 24. If the offender is over 16 the maximum number of hours is 36: PCC(S)A 2000 s.60(4).

Aged 16–25: The court must not make an attendance centre order unless it is satisfied that the attendance centre to be specified is reasonably accessible to the person concerned, having regard to his age, the means of access available to him, and any other circumstances.

The court cannot require an individual to attend an attendance centre on more than one occasion per day and for more than three hours on any occasion: PCC(S)A 2000 s.60(10).

Avoid conflict with school/work/religious beliefs: The times at which the offender is required to attend shall be such as to avoid interference, so far as is practicable, with the offender's school hours or working hours: PCC(S)A 2000 s.60(7).

Breach

Magistrates' court (PCC(S)A 2000 Sch.5, para.2(1)): Breach of the requirements of an attendance centre order enables a magistrates' court to:

(a) impose a fine not exceeding £1,000,

(b) where the original order was made by a magistrates' court, re-sentence for the original offence (magistrates' court powers apply),

(c) where the original order was made by the Crown Court, commit him to custody or release him on bail until he can be brought before the Crown Court.

Crown Court (PCC(S)A 2000 Sch.5, para.3): Breach of the requirements of an attendance centre order enables a crown court to:

(a) deal with him in any way he could have been dealt with for the original offence

(b) revoke the order

(c) where the individual has wilfully and persistently failed to comply, impose a custodial sentence.

Commission of an offence while subject to an attendance centre order does not give rise to any power in respect of the attendance centre order.

Automatic Barring

SAFEGUARDING VULNERABLE GROUPS ACT 2006

References: Archbold 5–1123

Where a person is convicted of an offence which is prescribed for the purposes of the Safeguarding Vulnerable Groups Act 2006, the Disclosure and Barring Service must include his name in either the children's barred list or the adult's barred list. **The court before which the offender is convicted must inform the person at the time he is convicted that the Service will include him in the barred list concerned.** The court does not make any order in relation to inclusion in the barred lists.

The following are the offences in respect of which the offender is liable to be included in one or other or both of the barred lists:

Kidnapping (not false imprisonment);

Murder (not manslaughter);

Offences contrary to any of the following statutory provisions:

Asylum and Immigration Act 2004 s.4;

Child Abduction Act 1984 ss.1, 2, 6;

Children and Young Persons Act 1933 s.1;

Criminal Justice Act 1988 s.160;

Criminal Law Act 1977 s.54;

Customs and Excise Management Act 1979 s.170, where the goods concerned were prohibited by the Customs Consolidation Act 1876 s.42 (indecent or obscene articles);

Domestic Violence, Crime and Victims Act 2004 s.5;

Indecency with Children Act 1960 s.1;

Infanticide Act 1938 s.1;

Mental Capacity Act 2005 s.44;

Mental Health Act 1959 s.128;

Mental Health Act 1983 ss.126, 127, 128, 129;

Misuse of Drugs Act 1971 s.4(3), where the drugs were supplied or offered to a child;

Nationality, Immigration and Asylum Act 2002 s.145;

Offences against the Person Act 1861 s.21 **(not ss.18, 20, or 47);**

Protection of Children Act 1978 s.1;

Sexual Offences Act 1956, ss.1, 2, 3, 4, 6, 7, 9, 10, 11, 12, 13, 14, 15, 16, 17, 19, 20, 21, 22, 23, 24, 25, 26, 27, 28, 29, 30, 31;

Sexual Offences Act 1967, ss.4 and 5;

Sexual Offences (Amendment) Act 2000 s.3;

Sexual Offences Act 2003 ss.1, 2, 3, 4, 5, 6, 7, 8, 9, 10 ,11, 12, 14, 15, 16, 17, 18, 19, 20, 25, 26, 30, 31, 32, 33, 34, 35, 36, 37, 38, 39, 40, 41, 47, 48, 49, 50, 52, 53, 57, 58, 59, 61, 62, 63, 66, 67;

Theft Act 1968 s.9(1)(a) (where the offence was committed with intent to commit rape);

Any "connected offence" of the listed offences.

"Connected offence" means any offence of attempting, conspiring or incitement to commit that offence, or aiding, abetting, counselling or procuring the commission of the offence.

It is uncertain whether the reference to incitement in this provision includes a reference to offences contrary to the Serious Crime Act 2007 ss.44, 45 and 46.

Note: offences contrary to the law of Scotland and Northern Ireland, and to the Armed Forces Act 2006 or earlier service legislation, are omitted. References to statutory provisions replaced by the Sexual Offences Act 1956 are omitted.

Automatic Deportation

UK Borders Act 2007 s.32

References: Archbold 5–1267

Note: only condition 1 of s.32 was in force on November 13, 2014

If a person aged 18 or over who is not a British citizen is convicted in the United Kingdom of an offence and sentenced to **at least 12 months' imprisonment or detention in a young offender institution**, the Secretary of State must make a deportation order unless the order would breach the person's convention rights, the United Kingdom's obligations under the Refugee Convention or the rights of the person under the Community treaties. Certain other categories of persons are also exempt from automatic deportation. The fact that a person is exempt from automatic deportation does not prevent the Secretary of State from making a deportation order in the exercise of his discretion.

A person who is sentenced to a suspended sentence of imprisonment or detention in a young offender institution does not qualify for automatic deportation unless the sentence is *subsequently activated in whole or part.*

A person who is sentenced to a period of imprisonment or detention in a young offender institution for at least 12 months only by virtue of being sentenced to consecutive sentences amounting in aggregate to **12 months or more** *does not qualify for automatic deportation.* A court should not reduce the length of an otherwise appropriate sentence in order to avoid the offender becoming liable to automatic deportation.

The sentencing court has no power to make any order in connection with these provisions. A court should not make a recommendation for deportation in the case of an offender who is liable for automatic deportation.

Banning Orders

FOOTBALL SPECTATORS ACT 1989 s.14

References: Current Sentencing Practice H6–1; Archbold 5–1067

If an offender is convicted of a **relevant offence** and the court is satisfied that there are *reasonable grounds to believe that a banning order would help to prevent violence or disorder at or in connection with any regulated football matches*, it **must** make a banning order. If the court is not so satisfied, it **must** state that fact in open court and give its reasons.

A banning order prohibits the offender from attending a regulated football match in England and Wales, and requires him to report when required to a police station when football matches are being played outside England and Wales. A banning order may include other requirements. The order must require the offender to surrender his passport in connection with matches played outside England and Wales.

If the offender is sentenced to custody, the banning order must be for at least six years and not more than 10 years.

If the offender is not sentenced to custody, the banning order must be for at least three years and not more than five years.

A banning order may be made only in addition to any other form of sentence or in addition to a discharge.

The following offences are relevant offences:

(a) any offence under the Football Spectators Act 1989 ss.14J(1) or 21C(2);

(b) any offence under ss.2 or 2A of the Sporting Events (Control of Alcohol, etc.) Act 1985 (alcohol, containers and fireworks) committed by the accused at any regulated football match or while entering or trying to enter the ground;

(c) any offence under **s.4A** or s.5 of the Public Order Act 1986 (harassment, alarm or distress) or any provision of Pt III of that Act (racial hatred) committed during a period relevant to a regulated football match at any premises while the accused was at, or was entering or leaving or trying to enter or leave, the premises;

(d) **any offence involving the use or threat of violence by the accused towards another person committed during a period** relevant to a regulated football match at any premises while the accused was at, or was entering or leaving or trying to enter or leave, the premises;

(e) **any offence involving the use or threat of violence towards property committed during a period relevant to a regulated football match at any premises while the accused was at, or was entering or leaving or trying to enter or leave, the premises;**

(f) any offence involving *the use, carrying or possession of an offensive weapon or a firearm* committed during a period relevant to a regulated football match at any premises while the accused was at, or was entering or leaving or trying to enter or leave, the premises;

(g) any offence under s.12 of the Licensing Act 1872 (persons found drunk in public places, etc.) of being found drunk in a highway or other public place committed while the accused was on a journey to or from a regulated football match applies in respect of which the court makes a declaration of relevance;

(h) any offence under s.91(1) of the Criminal Justice Act 1967 (disorderly behaviour while drunk in a public place) committed in a highway or other public place while the accused was on a journey to or from a regulated football match in respect of which the court makes a declaration of relevance;

(i) any offence under s.1 of the Sporting Events (Control of Alcohol, etc.) Act 1985 (alcohol on coaches or trains to or from sporting events) committed while the accused was on a journey to or from a regulated football match in respect of which the court makes a declaration of relevance;

(j) any offence under **s.4A or s.5 of the Public Order Act 1986** (harassment, alarm or distress) or any provision of Pt III of that Act (racial hatred) committed while the accused was on a journey to or from a regulated football match in respect of which the court makes a declaration of relevance;

(k) any offence under ss.4 or 5 of the Road Traffic Act 1988 (driving, etc. when under the influence of drink or drugs or with an alcohol concentration above the prescribed limit) committed while the accused was on a journey to or from a regulated football match in respects of which the court makes a declaration of relevance;

(l) **any offence involving the use or threat of violence by the accused towards another person committed while one or each of them was on a journey to or from a regulated football match in respect of which the court makes a declaration of relevance;**

(m) **any offence involving the use or threat of violence towards property committed while the accused was on a journey to or**

from a regulated football match in respect of which the court makes a declaration of relevance;

(n) **any offence involving the use, carrying or possession of an offensive weapon or a firearm committed while the accused was on a journey to or from a regulated football match in respect of which the court makes a declaration of relevance;**

(o) any offence under the Football (Offences) Act 1991;

(p) any other offence under **s.4A or s.5 of the Public Order Act 1986** (harassment, alarm or distress) or any provision of Pt III of that Act (racial hatred) which was committed during a period relevant to a regulated football match in respect of which the court makes a declaration that the offence related to that match or to that match and any other football match which took place during that period;

(q) **any other offence involving the use or threat of violence by the accused towards another person which was committed during a period relevant to a regulated football match in respect of which the court makes a declaration that the offence related to that match or to that match and any other football match which took place during that period;**

(r) any other offence involving the use or threat of violence towards property which was committed during a period relevant to a regulated football match in respect of which the court makes a declaration that the offence related to that match or to that match and any other football match which took place during that period;

(s) any other offence involving the use, carrying or possession of an offensive weapon which was committed during a period relevant to a regulated football match in respect of which the court makes a declaration that the offence related to that match or to that match and any other football match which took place during that period;

(t) any offence under s.166 of the Criminal Justice and Public Order Act 1994 (sale of tickets by unauthorised persons) which relates to tickets for a football match.

The **period relevant** to a football match is the period beginning 24 hours before the start of the match, or the advertised start, and ending 24 hours after the end of the match. If the match does not take place, the period is the period beginning 24 hours before the time at which it was advertised to start, and ending 24 hours after that time.

*The court may not make a **declaration of relevance** unless the prosecutor gave notice to the defendant five days before the first day of the trial that it was proposed to show that the offence related to football matches, unless the offender consents to waive* *the requirement or the court is satisfied that the interests of justice do not require more notice to be given.*

A regulated football match is an association football match in which one or both of the participating teams represents a club which is for the time being a member (whether a full or associate member) of the Football League, the Football Association Premier League or the Football Conference, or represents a club from outside England and Wales, or represents a country or territory; and which is either played at a sports ground which is designated by order under s.1(1) of the Safety of Sports Grounds Act 1975, or registered with the Football League or the Football Association Premier League as the home ground of a club which is a member of the Football League or the Football Association Premier League at the time the match is played; or is played in the Football Association Cup (other than in a preliminary or qualifying round).

The prosecution may appeal against the failure of a court to make a banning order.

Binding Over

JUSTICES OF THE PEACE ACT 1968 s.1(7)

References: Current Sentencing Practice D10–1; Archbold 5–177

A person who has been convicted of an offence may be bound over to come up for judgment when called, on such conditions as the court may specify.

A person "who or whose case" is before the Crown Court or a magistrates' court may be bound over to keep the peace and to be of good behaviour, whether or not he has been charged with or convicted of an offence.

A witness who has not given evidence is not liable to be bound over.

A person who has not been charged with an offence should not be bound over without being given the opportunity to make representations before being bound over.

A person who refuses to be bound over may be committed to prison. A person under 18 may consent to be bound over, but may not be committed to custody if he refuses to be bound over.

Where a court proposes to bind over a person in a substantial amount, it should allow him to address the court on the amount.

Where a person is bound over to keep the peace and be of good behaviour, there is no power to insert additional specific conditions.

Where a person who has been bound over to keep the peace and be of good behaviour fails to comply with the terms of the binding over, he is liable to be ordered to pay the amount in which he has been bound over, but cannot be sentenced to custody.

Committal for Sentence

P.C.C.(S.)A. 2000 ss.3–7 (as amended by Criminal Justice Act 2003 Sch.3)

References: Current Sentencing Practice L12–1A01, Archbold 5–25

Adult offenders (section 3)

Where an offender aged 18 or over is convicted on summary trial of an offence triable either way, he may be committed to the Crown Court for sentence, either in custody or on bail, if the court by which he is convicted is of the opinion that the offence or the combination of the offence and one or more offences associated with it was so serious that the Crown Court should, in the court's opinion, have the power to deal with the offender in any way in which it could deal with him if he had been convicted on indictment.

(This provision does not apply to offences where the section is excluded by reference to the value of the property involved.)

A person committed for sentence under this provision may be dealt with by the Crown Court in any way in which the Crown Court could deal with him if he had just been convicted of the offence on the indictment.

Dangerous adult offenders (section 3A)

Where an offender aged 18 or over is convicted on a summary trial of an either-way offence which is a specified offence for the purposes of the Criminal Justice Act 2003 Sch.15 and it appears to the court that the criteria for the imposition of an extended sentence under the Criminal Justice Act 2003 s.226A are met, the court must commit the offender either in custody or on bail to the Crown Court for sentence.

In reaching any decision or their taking any steps under this section, the court shall not be bound by any indication of sentence given in respect of the offence under the Magistrates' Courts Act 1980 s.20, and nothing the court does under this section may be challenged or be the subject of any appeal in any court on the ground that it is not consistent with an indication of sentence.

A person committed for sentence under this provision may be dealt with by the Crown Court in any way in which the Crown Court could deal with him if he had just been convicted of the offence on the indictment.

Related offences (section 4)

If a magistrates' court has sent an offender aged 18 or over for trial for some offences, but has to deal with the offender for other either-way offences in relation to which he has indicated an intention to plead guilty, the magistrates' court may commit the defendant to the Crown Court for sentence for those offences, provided that they are offences which could be included in the same indictment as the first offences.

The offender may be committed for sentence even though the court is not satisfied that greater punishment should be inflicted for those offences than the magistrates' court has power to inflict.

If the offender has indicated an intention to plead guilty to certain offences, but the magistrates' court has not yet determined whether to send the offender to the Crown Court for trial in respect of related offences, the magistrates' court must adjourn the proceedings in relation to the offences in respect of which the offender has indicated an intention to plead guilty, and if it sends the offender to the Crown Court for trial for the related offence or offences, it may then commit him for sentence.

If the magistrates' court commits an offender under this provision, it should state whether it has power also to commit the offender under the P.C.C.(S.)A. 2000 s.3.

If the offender is convicted of the offences for which he has been sent for trial, or if the magistrates' court on committing him for sentence has stated that it has power to commit him for sentence for the other offences under the P.C.C.(S.)A. 2000 s.3, the Crown Court may impose any sentence for the offences for which he has been committed for sentence which it would have power to impose if the offender had just been convicted on indictment.

If the defendant is not convicted of those offences for which he has been sent for trial, and the magistrates' court has not stated that it had power to commit him under the P.C.C.(S.)A. 2000 s.3, the Crown Court must deal with the offender for the offences for which he has been committed for sentence in a manner in which the magistrates' court could deal with him if it had just convicted him.

This procedure should not be used unless the defendant has been sent for trial for related offences. A defendant who has been convicted by a magistrates' court after indicating an intention to plead guilty in other circumstances should be committed under s.3.

Young offenders

Indictated plea (section 3B)

Where a person aged under 18 appears before a magistrates' court on an information charging him with **an offence in respect of which the sentencing court would have power to impose a term of detention under the P.C.C.(S.)A. 2000 s.91(1)**, and the person indicates that he would plead guilty if the offence were to proceed to trial and the court convicts him, and the court is of the opinion that the offence and the combination of the offence and one or more offences associated with it was such that the Crown Court should in the court's opinion have power to deal with the offender as if the provisions of the P.C.C.(S.)A. 2000 s.91 applied, the court may commit him in custody or on bail to the Crown Court for sentence.

In considering the associated offence it is submitted that the magistrates' court is not limited to the consideration of offences in respect of which the sentencing court would have power to impose a term of detention under the P.C.C.(S.)A. 2000 s.91(1).

A person committed for sentence under this provision may be dealt with by the Crown Court in any way in which the Crown Court could deal with him if he had just been convicted of the offence on the indictment.

This provision does not apply to an offender convicted following a contested summary trial of an offence in respect of which the sentencing court would have power to impose a term of detention under the P.C.C.(S.)A. 2000 s.91(1).

Dangerous young defendant (section 3C)

A defendant under 18 who has been convicted by a magistrates' court of a specified offence **must** be committed to the Crown Court if the court considers that there is a significant risk of serious harm to the public caused by further specified offences committed by him, and that the criteria for the imposition of an extended sentence of detention would be met.

Where a young defendant is committed for sentence under this provision the Crown Court may deal with the offender in any way in which it could deal with him if he had just been convicted of the offence on indictment before the court. The Crown Court is not bound to deal with the defendant under the Criminal Justice Act 2003 s.266B, unless it considers that there is a significant risk of serious harm to the public caused by further specified offences committed by him. If it does not so consider, the Crown Court may impose any other sentence which is open to the court for an offender of the defendant's age.

The age of the defendant for the purpose of determining the sentencing powers of the Crown Court is his age on the date on which he was convicted. If a defendant is convicted by a magistrates' court at the age of 17 and is committed for sentence, but attains the age of 18 before he appears before the Crown Court, the Crown Court must deal with him as a 17-year-old.

Related offences (section 4A)

If a magistrates' court has sent an offender aged under 18 for trial for some offences, but has to deal with the offender for other related offences in respect of which **the sentencing court would have power to impose a term of detention under the P.C.C.(S.)A. 2000 s.91(1)**, in respect of which he has indicated that he would plead guilty if the offence were to proceed to trial, the court may commit him in custody or on bail to the Crown Court for sentence.

This procedure does not apply to offences in respect of which the sentencing court would not have power to impose a term of detention under the P.C.C.(S.)A. 2000 s.91(1).

The offender may be committed for sentence even though the court is not satisfied that greater punishment should be inflicted for those offences than the magistrates' court has power to inflict.

If the offender has indicated an intention to plead guilty to certain offences, but the magistrates' court has not yet determined whether to send the offender to the Crown Court for trial in respect of related offences, the magistrates' court must adjourn the proceedings in relation to the offences in respect of which the offender has indicated an intention to plead guilty, and if it sends the offender to the Crown Court for trial for the related offence or offences, it may then commit him for sentence.

If the magistrates' court commits an offender under this provision, it should state whether it has power also to commit the offender under the P.C.C.(S.)A. 2000 ss.3B or 3C.

If the offender is convicted of the offences for which he has been sent for trial, or if the magistrates' court on committing him for sentence has stated that it has power to commit him for sentence for the other offences under the P.C.C.(S.)A. 2000 ss.3B or 3C, the Crown Court may impose any sentence for the offences for which he has been committed for sentence which it would have power to impose if the offender had just been convicted on indictment.

If the defendant is not convicted of those offences for which he has been sent for trial, and the magistrates' court has not stated that it had power to commit him under the P.C.C.(S.)A. 2000 ss.3B or 3C, the Crown Court must deal with the offender for the offences for which he has been committed for sentence in a manner in which the magistrates' court could deal with him if it had just convicted him.

This procedure should not be used unless the defendant has been sent for trial for related offences. A defendant who has been convicted by a magistrates' court after indicating an intention to plead guilty in other circumstances should be committed under ss.3B or 3C in relation to the offences to which those sections apply.

Subsidiary offences (s.6)

Where an offender is committed for sentence under any of these provisions, or various other provisions relating to existing sentences, the magistrates' court may commit the offender for other offences for which he could not be committed under the principal provision. The offence must be punishable with imprisonment, or with disqualification from driving under ss.34, 35 or 36 of the Road Traffic Offenders Act 1988, or be a suspended sentence in respect of which the magistrates' court has power to deal with the offender. The power may be exercised in conjunction with other powers of committal. The section does not apply in the case of an offender subject to a community order made under the Criminal Justice Act 2003 who is committed to the Crown Court under the Criminal Justice Act 2003 Sch.8, para.22, following his conviction by a magistrates' court of an offence while a community order made by the Crown Court is in force.

Where an offender is committed under s.6, the Crown Court must observe all limits which would apply to a magistrates' court passing sentence for those offences, both in relation to the maximum term of imprisonment which the magistrates' court may pass for the individual offences, and the limitations on the aggregate maximum term of imprisonment which the magistrates' court may impose for all the offences. See **Magistrates' Courts Powers—Custodial Sentences**.

Defective committals

Where an offender is committed to the Crown Court for sentence, and it is alleged that the committal is unlawful for want of jurisdiction or otherwise, the normal remedy is by way of judicial review. The Crown Court may decline to pass sentence only if the committal is obviously bad on its face.

The Crown Court has no power to remit the case to the magistrates' court where it appears that the defendant is not guilty of the offence for which he had been committed, but it may allow him to withdraw or change his plea and then remit the case to the magistrates' court.

Community Orders—Criminal Justice Act 2003— Breaches of Orders and Re-offending

CRIMINAL JUSTICE ACT 2003 SCH.8

References: Current Sentencing Practice D14–1; Archbold 5–339

Breach of requirement of order

Where it is proved to a magistrates' court that an offender subject to a community order has failed without reasonable excuse to comply with any of the requirements of the relevant order, the court must either:

(a) impose more onerous requirements than the original order; or

(b) if the failure to comply took place on or after December 3, 2012, impose a fine not exceeding £2,500; or

(c) if the order was made by a magistrates' court, deal with him, for the offence in respect of which the order was made, *in any manner in which it could deal with him if he had just been convicted by the court of the offence.*

In dealing with the offender, the court must take into account the extent to which the offender has complied with the requirements of the relevant order. If the offender has wilfully and persistently failed to comply with the order, the court may pass a custodial sentence, whether or not the other criteria for a custodial sentence are satisfied.

If the magistrates' court deals with the offender for the offence, it must revoke the order.

If the community order was made by the Crown Court, the magistrates' court may commit the offender to the Crown Court, as an alternative to imposing more onerous requirements.

When the offender appears before the Crown Court, the breach of the order must be proved to the satisfaction of the Crown Court. If the breach is proved, the Crown Court must:

(a) impose more onerous requirements than the original order contained; or

(b) if the failure to comply took place on or after December 3, 2012, impose a fine not exceeding £2,500; or

(c) deal with him, for the offence in respect of which the order was made, *in any manner in which he could have been dealt with by the court which made the original order if the order had not been made.*

In dealing with the offender, the court must take into account the extent to which the offender has complied with the requirements of the relevant order.

If the offender has wilfully and persistently failed to comply with the order, the court may pass a custodial sentence, whether or not the other criteria for a custodial sentence are satisfied.

If the court deals with the offender for the offence, it must revoke the order.

Commission of further offence

If an offender in respect of whom a community order made by a magistrates' court is in force is convicted by magistrates' court, and the magistrates' court considers it in the interests of justice to do so, the magistrates' court may either simply revoke the community order, or revoke the order and deal with the offender in any way in which he could have been dealt with by the court which made the order.

If an offender in respect of whom a community order made by the Crown Court is in force is convicted by magistrates' court, the magistrates' court may commit the offender to the Crown Court.

If an offender appears before the Crown Court having been committed by the magistrates' court following a conviction by the magistrates' court, or if the offender is convicted of an offence before the Crown Court while he is subject to a community order, whether the order was made by the magistrates' court or by the Crown Court, the Crown Court may either revoke the order, or revoke the order and deal with the order in any way in which he could have been dealt with by the court which made the order.

The power to deal with the offender depends on his being convicted while the order is still in force; it does not arise where he is convicted after the order has expired of an offence committed while the order was current.

The offender must be sentenced on the basis of his age when the original order was made, not on his age at the date of sentence. If the offender is convicted before the Crown Court while he is subject to a community order made by a magistrates' court, the Crown Court may impose only a sentence which would have been open to the magistrates' court which convicted him.

In sentencing the offender, the Crown Court must take account of the extent to which he has complied with the requirements of the order.

Community Orders—Criminal Justice Act 2003—General Criteria and Requirements

References: Current Sentencing Practice D13–1; Archbold 5–185

Availability

Power: Where a person aged 18 or over is convicted of an offence, subject to the restrictions set out below, the court may make a community order imposing one or more requirements (see below): CJA 2003 s.177(1).

Test to apply *(CJA 2003 s.148(1) and (2))*: A court may not impose a community sentence unless it is of the opinion that:

(a) the offence or the combination of the offence and one or more offences associated with the offence are **"serious enough to warrant such a sentence"**;

(b) the particular requirements or combination of requirements are **"the most suitable for the offender"**; and

(c) the restrictions on liberty imposed by the order are **"commensurate with the seriousness of the offence"** or the combination of offences for which the sentence is imposed.

The fact that the offence is serious enough to warrant a community order, or the proposed requirements are commensurate with the seriousness of the offence or the combination of offences for which the order would be imposed, does not mean that the court is required to make a community order or to impose those restrictions: CJA 2003 s.148(5).

No power to make community order *(CJA 2003 s.150(1) and (2))*: A community order is not exercisable in respect of an offence for which:

(a) the sentence is fixed by law, or

(b) a custodial sentence must be imposed under:

    (i) s.51A(2) of the Firearms Act 1968 (minimum sentence for certain firearms offences),

    (ii) ss.110(2) or 111(2) of the Sentencing Act (minimum sentence for third domestic burglary or drug trafficking offence),

    (iii) s.29(4) or (6) of the Violent Crime Reduction Act 2006 (minimum sentence for offence of using someone to mind a weapon),

(iv) s.224A of the Criminal Justice Act 2003 (automatic life sentence),

(v) s.225(2) or 226(2) of the Criminal Justice Act 2003 (requirement to impose sentence of imprisonment for life or detention for life),

(vi) s.1A(5) of the Prevention of Crime Act 1953 (minimum sentence for offence of threatening with offensive weapon in public), or

(vii) s.139AA(7) of the Criminal Justice Act 1988 (minimum sentence for offence of threatening with article with blade or point in public or on school premises or with offensive weapon on school premises).

Offence must carry imprisonment: A community order may not be made in respect of an offence which is not punishable with imprisonment: CJA 2003 s.150A(1)(a).

Making the order

Punitive element: The order **must** include at least one requirement imposed for the purpose of punishment, or impose a fine for the offence in respect of which the community order is made, or both: CJA 2003 s.177(2A). That obligation does not apply where the court is of the view that there are exceptional circumstances which relate to the offender which would make it unjust to impose a requirement for the purposes of punishment and/or a fine: CJA 2003 s.177(2B).

Maximum length: A community order must specify a date, not more than three years after the date of the order, by which all the requirements must have been complied with: CJA 2003 s.177(5).

Where the court imposes two or more requirements, it may specify a date by which each of those requirements must be completed, the last of which must be the end date of the order (not more than three years after the order was made): CJA 2003 s.177(5A).

Discount for time on remand: Where the court makes a community order in respect of an offender who has previously been remanded in custody, it may have regard to any period during which the offender has been remanded in custody in connection with the offence for which the order is made, or any offence founded on the same facts or evidence, in determining the restrictions on liberty to be imposed on the offender. The court has a discretion; there is no obligation to make any allowance in the terms of the order for time spent in custody on remand: CJA 2003 s.149.

Local justice area: A community order must specify the local justice area in which the offender resides or will reside: CJA 2003 s.216.

Copies of the order: These must be given to the offender, and to an officer of a local probation board or (in the case of an offender under 18) either an officer of a local probation board or a member of a youth offending team, and to others concerned with the operation of the order: CJA 2003 s.219.

Breach: The Crown Court may include in the order a direction that any breach of the order is to be dealt with by a magistrates' court. If no such direction is made, any breach will be dealt with by the Crown Court.

Requirements

There is no restriction on the requirements which may be combined in the same community order, but the court must consider whether the requirements are compatible with each other, CJA 2003 s.177(6).

The requirements of a community order shall, as far as is practicable, avoid any conflict with the offender's religious beliefs or the requirements of any other community order to which he may be subject, and any interference with the times at which he normally works, or attends school or an educational establishment, CJA 2003 s.217.

Activity requirements *(CJA 2003 s.201)*: An activity requirement requires the offender either to present himself to a person or persons specified in the order at a place or places specified on such number of days as may be specified, or to participate in activities specified in the order on the number of days specified: CJA 2003 s.201(1).

An activity requirement may not be included in an order unless the court has consulted an officer of a local probation board and is satisfied that it is "feasible to secure compliance with the requirement": CJA 2003 s.218(2).

The aggregate of the number of days on which the offender may be required to present himself to a person or participate in activities must not exceed 60: CJA 2003 s.201(5).

A court may not include an activity requirement in a relevant order if compliance with that requirement would involve the co-operation of a person other than the offender and the offender's responsible officer, unless that other person consents to its inclusion: CJA 2003 s.201(4).

Where the court imposes an activity requirement, it may also impose an electronic monitoring requirement (see below): CJA 2003 s.177(4).

***Alcohol abstinence and monitoring requirement** (CJA 2003 s.212A) (in force on 31 July 2014 in relation to the south London justice area only)*: An alcohol abstinence and monitoring requirement is a requirement that, subject to such exceptions as are specified, the offender must abstain from consuming alcohol throughout a specified period, or must not consume alcohol during a specified period so that the level of alcohol in the offender's body does not exceed a specified amount: CJA 2003 s.212A(1)(a).

The specified period **must not exceed 120 days**: CJA 2003 s.212A(2).

An alcohol abstinence and monitoring requirement may not be made unless:

(i) the consumption of alcohol is an element of the offence for which the order is to be imposed, or of an associated offence;

(ii) the court is satisfied that the offender is not dependent on alcohol;

(iii) the order does not include an alcohol treatment requirement; and

(iv) the court has been informed that arrangements for monitoring the requirement are available. (CJA 2003 s.212A(8)–(12).)

If the requirement is that the offender must not consume alcohol during a specified period so that the level of alcohol in the offender's body does not exceed a specified amount, the amount specified must be the amount prescribed by the Secretary of State: CJA 2003 s.212A(4).

The offender must submit to monitoring in accordance with arrangements specified by the Secretary of State: CJA 2003 s.212A(1)(b). An alcohol abstinence and monitoring requirement may not be made unless such arrangements are in force: CJA 2003 s.212A(6).

Alcohol treatment requirements: An alcohol treatment requirement is a requirement that the offender must submit during a period specified in the order to treatment with a view to the reduction or elimination of the offender's dependency on alcohol: CJA 2003 s.212(1).

An alcohol treatment requirement may be made if the court is satisfied that the offender:

(i) is dependent on alcohol, and

(ii) that his dependency is such as requires, and may be susceptible to, treatment, and

(iii) that arrangements have been or can be made for the treatment intended to be specified in the order (including arrangements for the reception of the offender where he is to be required to submit to treatment as a resident). (CJA 2003 s.212(2).)

The court may not include or make an alcohol treatment requirement unless the offender expresses his willingness to comply with the requirement: CJA 2003 s.212(3).

The treatment required by the alcohol treatment requirement must be:

(i) treatment as a resident in such institution or place as may be specified in the order,

(ii) treatment as a non-resident in such institution or place at such intervals as may be specified in the order, or

(iii) treatment by or under the direction of a qualified person specified in the order. (CJA 2003 s.212(5).)

The court may not make an alcohol treatment requirement unless it is satisfied that arrangements have been made for the proposed treatment, including arrangements for the offender's reception where he is required to submit to treatment as a resident: CJA 2003 s.212(2)(c).

Where the court imposes an alcohol treatment requirement, it may also impose an electronic monitoring requirement (see below): CJA 2003 s.177(4).

Attendance centre requirements *(CJA 2003 s.214)*: An attendance centre requirement may be made in respect of an offender under 25: CJA 2003 s.177(1)(l). It requires the offender to attend an attendance centre for a number of hours specified in the order: CJA 2003 s.214(1).

The order must be for a total of not less than 12 hours and not more than 36 hours: CJA 2003 s.214(2).

The court must not make an attendance centre requirement unless it is satisfied that the attendance centre to be specified is reasonably accessible to the person concerned, having regard to the means of access available to him, and any other circumstances: CJA 2003 s.214(3).

The offender must not be required to attend at an attendance centre on more than one occasion on any one day, or for more than three hours on any occasion: CJA 2003 s.214(6).

A court may not include an attendance centre requirement in a relevant order in respect of an offender unless the court has been notified by the Secretary of State that an attendance centre is available for persons of his description: CJA 2003 s.218(3).

Where the court imposes an attendance centre requirement, it may also impose an electronic monitoring requirement (see below): CJA 2003 s.177(4).

Curfew requirements *(CJA 2003 s.204)*: A curfew requirement requires the offender to remain, for periods specified in the requirement, at a place specified in the order: CJA 2003 s.204(1).

The periods specified must be not less than two hours and not more than 16 hours (12 hours if the offence was committed before December 3, 2012) in any day: CJA 2003 s.204(2).

The requirement may specify different places or different periods for different days.

All the specified periods must fall within the period of twelve months (six months if the offence was committed before December 3, 2012) beginning with the day on which the order is made: CJA 2003 s.204(3).

Before making a curfew requirement, the court must obtain and consider information about the place to be specified in the order and the attitude of persons likely to be affected by the enforced presence there of the offender: CJA 2003 s.204(6).

The court **must** impose an electronic monitoring requirement unless a person whose co-operation is necessary does not consent, or the court has not been notified that arrangements for electronic monitoring are available, or in the particular circumstances of the case the court considers it inappropriate to do so: CJA 2003 s.177(3).

Drug rehabilitation requirements *(CJA 2003 s.209)*: A drug rehabilitation requirement requires the offender to submit, during the treatment and testing period, to treatment by a specified person with a view to the reduction or elimination of the offender's dependency on or propensity to misuse drugs: CJA 2003 s.209(1)(a). The requirement must also require the offender to provide samples during the treatment and testing period at times and in circumstances determined by a responsible officer or person providing treatment, for the purpose of ascertaining whether he has any drug in his body during the treatment and testing period: CJA 2003 s.209(1)(b).

The treatment must be treatment as a resident in a specified institution or place, or treatment as a non-resident in a specified institution or place: CJA 2003 s.209(4). The nature of the treatment is not specified in the order: CJA 2003 s.209(4).

A drug rehabilitation requirement may be made only if the court is satisfied that:

(i)   the offender is dependent on or has a propensity to misuse drugs;

(ii) his dependency or propensity is such as requires and may be susceptible to treatment,

(iii) arrangements have been or can be made for the treatment intended to be specified in the order,

(iv) the requirement has been recommended by an officer of a local probation board, and

(v)   **the offender has expressed his willingness to comply with the requirement**. (CJA 2003 s.209(2).)

A drug rehabilitation requirement may (and must if the treatment and testing period is more than 12 months) provide for the order to be reviewed periodically at intervals of not less than one month at a hearing held for the purpose by the court responsible for the order. The offender may be required to attend each review hearing (and must if the period is more than 12 months).

A drug rehabilitation requirement may (and must if the treatment and testing period is more than 12 months)—

(a) provide for the requirement to be reviewed periodically at intervals of not less than one month,

(b) provide for each review of the requirement to be made at a hearing held for the purpose by the court responsible for the order (a "review hearing"),

(c) require the offender to attend each review hearing,

(d) provide for a probation officer to produce a report in writing on the offender's progress under the requirement before each review, and

(e) provide for each report to include the test results (under s.209(6)) and the views of the treatment provider as to the treatment and testing of the offender. (CJA 2003 s.210(1).)

At a review hearing the court, after considering the responsible officer's report, may amend any requirement or provision of the order: CJA 2003 s.211(1). The court may not amend the treatment or testing requirement unless the offender expresses his willingness to comply with the amended requirement: CJA 2003 s.211(2)(a).

If the offender fails to express his willingness to comply with the amended order, the court may revoke the order, and deal with him, for the offence in respect of which the order was made, in any manner in which it could deal with him if he had just been convicted by the court of the offence: CJA 2003 s.211(3). Partial compliance will be taken into account when dealing with the offender under s.211(3): CJA 2003 s.211(4). A custodial sentence may only be imposed where one was available for the original offence: CJA 2003 s.211(4).

If at a review hearing the court is of the opinion that the offender's progress under the order is satisfactory, the court may so amend the order as to provide for each subsequent review to be made by the court without a hearing, but this may be reversed: CJA 2003 s.211(6) and (7).

Where the court imposes a drug rehabilitation requirement, it may also impose an electronic monitoring requirement (see below): CJA 2003 s.177(4).

***Electronic monitoring requirements** (CJA 2003 s.215)*: An electronic monitoring requirement is a requirement for securing the electronic monitoring of the offender's compliance with other requirements imposed by the order: CJA 2003 s.215(1).

A court which makes a community order imposing an unpaid work requirement, an activity requirement, a programme requirement, a prohibited activity requirement, a residence requirement, a foreign travel prohibition requirement, a mental health treatment requirement, a drug rehabilitation requirement, an alcohol treatment requirement, a supervision requirement or an attendance centre requirement may also impose an electronic monitoring requirement: CJA 2003 s.177(4).

Where the court makes a community order imposing a curfew requirement or an exclusion requirement, the court must also impose an electronic monitoring requirement: CJA 2003 s.177(3).

An electronic monitoring requirement may not be included without the consent of any person without whose co-operation monitoring cannot be secured: CJA 2003 s.215(2).

An electronic monitoring requirement must include provision for making a person of a specified description responsible for the monitoring: CJA 2003 s.215(3).

An electronic monitoring requirement may be made only if the court has been notified that electronic monitoring requirements are available in the relevant areas and is satisfied that necessary provision can be made under those arrangements: CJA 2003 s.218(4).

***Exclusion requirements** (CJA 2003 s.205)*: An exclusion requirement prohibits the offender from entering any place specified in the order: CJA

2003 s.205(1). The requirement cannot exceed two years (whatever the length of the community order): CJA 2003 s.205(2). The prohibition may operate continuously or only during specified periods and different places may be specified in the order for different periods or days: CJA 2003 s.205(3).

The court **must** impose an electronic monitoring requirement unless a person whose co-operation is necessary does not consent, or the court has not been notified that arrangements for electronic monitoring are available, or in the particular circumstances of the case the court considers it inappropriate to do so: CJA 2003 s.177(3).

Foreign travel prohibition requirement *(CJA 2003 s.206A) (only available for offence committed on or after 3 December 2012)*: A foreign travel prohibition requirement may prohibit the offender from travelling to any country or territory outside the British Islands specified in the order, to any country or territory outside the British Islands not specified in the order, or to any country or territory outside the British Islands: CJA 2003 s.206A(1).

The requirement may apply to the day or days specified in the order, or for a period specified in the order: CJA 2003 s.206A(1).

The period specified may not exceed 12 months beginning with the day on which the order is made, and the day or days specified may not fall outside the period of 12 months beginning with the day on which the order is made: CJA 2003 s.206A(2) and (3).

Where the court imposes a foreign travel prohibition requirement, it may also impose an electronic monitoring requirement (see above): CJA 2003 s.177(4).

Mental health treatment requirements *(CJA 2003 s.207)*: A mental health treatment requirement is a requirement that the offender must submit, during a period or periods specified in the order, to treatment by or under the direction of a registered medical practitioner or a registered psychologist with a view to the improvement of the offender's mental condition: CJA 2003 s.207(1).

A court may not include a mental health treatment requirement in an order unless:

(a) it is satisfied:

   (i) that the mental condition of the offender is such as requires and is susceptible to treatment, but

   (ii) does not warrant his detention under a hospital order,

(b) **the offender has expressed his willingness to comply with the order**, and

(c) arrangements have been or can be made for the proposed treatment, including arrangements for the offender's reception as a resident patient, where treatment as a resident is proposed, CJA 2003 s.207(3).

The requirement relating to treatment may be for the whole period of the order, or for any part of the period of the order.

The treatment required by the order may be either treatment as a resident patient in an independent hospital or care home, or a hospital under the Mental Health Act 1983, other than a hospital where high-security services are provided, or treatment as a non-resident patient at such institution or place as may be specified in the order, or treatment by or under the direction of a medical practitioner or chartered psychologist specified in the order: CJA 2003 s.207(2).

The medical nature of the treatment is not specified in the order: CJA 2003 s.207(2).

Where the court imposes a mental health treatment requirement, it may also impose an electronic monitoring requirement (see above): CJA 2003 s.177(4).

Programme requirements: Repealed by LASPOA 2012 on December 3, 2012; see the 2014 edition of this work for details.

Prohibited activity requirements (CJA 2003 s.203): A prohibited activity requirement requires the offender to refrain from participating in activities specified in the requirement on a day or days specified in the order or during a period specified in the requirement: CJA 2003 s.203(1). The primary purpose is not to punish but to prevent—or at least reduce—further offending: *R. v J* [2008] EWCA Crim 2002.

A prohibited activity requirement may not be included in an order unless the court has consulted an officer of a local probation board: CJA 2003 s.203(2).

The prohibited activity requirements may include requirements relating to possessing, carrying or using firearms: CJA 2003 s.203(3).

Where the court imposes a prohibited activity requirement, it may also impose an electronic monitoring requirement (see above): CJA 2003 s.177(4).

Rehabilitation requirements *(not in force as at October 31, 2014)*: When s.15 of the Offender Rehabilitation Act 2014 is in force, s.200A will be added to the CJA 2003.

A "rehabilitation activity requirement" will be a requirement that, during the relevant period, the offender must comply with any instructions given by the responsible officer to attend appointments or participate in activities or both: CJA 2003 s.200A(1).

The activities in which offenders may be instructed to participate include activities forming an accredited programme (see s.202(2)) and activities whose purpose is reparative, such as restorative justice activities: CJA 2003 s.200A(7).

Residence requirements *(CJA 2003 s.206)*: A residence requirement is a requirement that, during a period specified in the relevant order, the offender must reside at a place specified in the order: CJA 2003 s.206(1).

Before making an order containing a residence requirement, the court must consider the home surroundings of the offender: CJA 2003 s.206(3).

The requirement may provide for the offender to reside at a place other than the place specified. A hostel or other institution may not be specified as the place of residence except on the recommendation of an officer of a local probation board: CJA 2003 s.206(2) and (4).

Where the court imposes a residence requirement, it may also impose an electronic monitoring requirement (see above): CJA 2003 s.177(4).

Supervision requirements: A supervision requirement may be made for the purpose of promoting the offender's rehabilitation. A supervision requirement requires the offender to attend appointments with the responsible officer.

Where the court imposes a supervision requirement, it may also impose an electronic monitoring requirement (see above): CJA 2003 s.177(4).

Unpaid work requirements *(CJA 2003 ss.199 and 200)*: An unpaid work requirement requires the offender to perform unpaid work for a number of hours, not less than 40 and not more than 300, specified in the order: CJA 2003 s.199(1).

An unpaid work requirement may not be made unless the court is satisfied that the offender is a suitable person to perform work under such a requirement: CJA 2003 s.199(3).

Where an offender is convicted of more than one offence, an unpaid work requirement may be made in respect of each offence, and may direct that the hours of work specified in any of the requirements should be concurrent with or in addition to the hours of work required by the other requirement, but the total number of hours which are not concurrent must not exceed the permissible maximum of 300: CJA 2003 s.199(5)

The work must normally be completed within 12 months, but the requirement remains in force until all the hours of work have been completed: CJA 2003 s.200(2) and (3).

It is not necessary for the offender to consent to the making of an unpaid work requirement: CJA 2003 s.199.

An unpaid work requirement is subject to the availability of local arrangements: CJA 2003 s.218(1).

Where the court imposes an unpaid work requirement, it may also impose an electronic monitoring requirement (see above): CJA 2003 s.177(4).

Offender's obligations

The offender must keep in touch with the responsible officer and notify him of any change of address: CJA 2003 s.220.

LIBRARY, UNIVERSITY OF CHESTER

Community Orders—Criminal Justice Act 2003— Offenders Previously Remanded in Custody

CRIMINAL JUSTICE ACT 2003 s.149

References: Current Sentencing Practice D13–1; Archbold 5–289

Note: these provisions apply only to community orders made under the Criminal Justice Act 2003.

Where a court makes a community order in respect of an offender who has previously been remanded in custody, it may have regard to any period during which the offender has been remanded in custody in connection with the offence for which the order is made, or any offence founded on the same facts or evidence, in determining the restrictions on liberty to be imposed on the offender.

The court has a discretion; there is no obligation to make any allowance in the terms of the order for time spent in custody on remand.

Compensation Order

P.C.C.(S.)A. 2000 s.130

References: Current Sentencing Practice J2–1; Archbold 5–691

A compensation order may be made in respect of any *personal injury, loss or damage* which results from an offence of which the offender is convicted or from any offence which is taken into consideration.

A compensation order may be made as the only sentence for an offence, or in addition to most other forms of sentence.

A court must consider making a compensation order in any case where it is empowered to do so. If the court has power to make a compensation order, but does not exercise the power, it must state its reasons for not doing so.

Magistrates' courts

A magistrates' court may order a maximum of £5,000 in respect of any one offence. If compensation is ordered to be paid in respect of offences taken into consideration, the total amount of the compensation must not exceed the total amount which the court could order in respect of all the offences of which the offender has been convicted (that is, £5,000 multiplied by the number of offences of which he has been convicted).

Death

Where a person has died as a result of an offence, a compensation order may be made for funeral expenses or bereavement in respect of death, except in the case of a death due to an accident arising out of the presence of a motor vehicle on a road. A compensation order in respect of funeral expenses may be made for the benefit of anyone who incurred the expenses. A compensation order in respect of bereavement may be made only for the benefit of a person for whose benefit a claim for damages for bereavement could be made under the Fatal Accidents Act 1976 s.1A. The amount of compensation in respect of bereavement must not exceed £11,800 (or £10,000 if the death occurred before January 1, 2008).

Road accidents

If personal injury, loss or damage arises out of an accident caused by the presence of a motor vehicle on a road, a compensation order may be made only if either *the damage can be treated as damage arising out of an offence under the Theft Act 1968* (this would include any damage to a vehicle which has been stolen or taken without consent, whoever has actually caused the damage, so long as the damage occurred while the vehicle was out of the owner's possession) or the offender is *uninsured in respect of the personal injury, loss or damage concerned and compensation is not payable under the Motor Insurer's Bureau Agreement*.

In practice the effect of this appears to be that a compensation order may not be made in respect of loss, damage or injury, unless the claimant was driving a vehicle which was itself not insured for the purposes of the Road Traffic Acts, or the claimant was a person who at the relevant time knew or ought to have known that the vehicle in which he was travelling had been stolen or unlawfully taken, or was not covered by insurance. In these cases the claimant is not covered by the MIB Agreement and the court may make a compensation order for the full amount of the loss, damage or personal injury. The court may also make a compensation order in favour of a claimant claiming by virtue of a right of subrogation.

General

The court must be satisfied that the injury, loss or damage which has occurred, is attributable to the offence in respect of which the compensation order is made.

The court must determine the amount of compensation which it considers appropriate, having regard to any evidence and to any representations that are made by or on behalf of the prosecutor.

If the value of the personal injury, loss or damage is not agreed by the defendant it must be established by evidence.

If the amount of the compensation due to the defendant cannot be established without complicated enquiries, it may be appropriate for the court to decline to make a compensation order and leave the victim to civil remedies.

A compensation order may be made in respect of a loss which is not itself actionable and may if appropriate contain an element of interest.

If the victim of an assault has provoked the assault by his own violent behaviour towards the offender, the amount of the compensation order may be reduced.

In determining whether to make a compensation order, or the amount of such an order, the **court must have regard to the means of the**

offender so far as they appear or are known to the court. *It is wrong in principle to impose a compensation order when there is no realistic possibility that the compensation will be paid within a reasonable time.*

If the compensation cannot be paid out of resources immediately available to the offender the court should determine the amount that he can reasonably pay out of income and order payment by instalments. The period of payment by instalments may extend to two years, or three years in exceptional circumstances.

The fact that the offender has been sentenced to custody does not necessarily mean that a compensation order is inappropriate, but a compensation order should not be made on the basis that the compensation will be paid out of future income unless the offender has clear prospects of employment on release from custody and the obligation to pay compensation will not be an encouragement to commit further offences.

If it is proposed to raise the necessary funds by selling assets, the court should satisfy itself that the assets do exist and should ensure that the assets have been valued by a competent person, before acting on the valuation. It is rarely appropriate to make a compensation order on the assumption that the necessary funds will be raised by the sale of the offender's matrimonial home.

The offender may be ordered to pay compensation even though he has not profited from the offence and his available assets are not themselves the proceeds of crime.

If the offender has been convicted of more than one offence, a separate order should be made in respect of each offence. If more than one offender has been convicted, a separate order should be made against each offender. If more than one offender has been convicted, but not all of them have the means to pay compensation, it is permissible to make an order against one offender for the whole amount of the loss, damage or injury.

The court does not fix any term of imprisonment in default, but may allow time for payment or fix payment by instalments.

If the amount of the compensation order exceeds £20,000, the Crown Court has power to enlarge the powers of the magistrates' court responsible for enforcing the order if it considers that the maximum default term of 12 months is inadequate. The court should make an order that the maximum term of imprisonment in default should be a figure taken from the table below:

Amount not exceeding:	Maximum term:
£50,000	18 months
£100,000	24 months
£250,000	36 months
£1 million	60 months
Over £1 million	120 months

If the court has made a confiscation order under Criminal Justice Act 1988 or the Proceeds of Crime Act 2002, the court should consider whether to make an order under Criminal Justice Act 1988 s.72(7) or the Proceeds of Crime Act 2002 s.13(6), which allows the court to direct that if the offender is unable to satisfy the compensation order because his means are inadequate, the deficiency shall be made good from the proceeds of the confiscation order.

Conditional Discharge

P.C.C.(S.)A. 2000 s.12

References: Current Sentencing Practice D11–1; Archbold 5–169

The court may grant a discharge for any offence other than murder or an offence in respect of which the court is obliged to pass a mandatory custodial sentence under the P.C.C.(S.)A. 2000 ss.109, 110 or 111, the Firearms Act 1968 s.51A, the Criminal Justice Act 2003 ss.225 or 226, the Prevention of Crime Act 1953 s.1A(5), the Violent Crime Reduction Act 2006 s.29 or the Criminal Justice Act 1988 s.139AA(7).

The court must be of the opinion, having regard to the circumstances including the nature of the offence and the character of the offender, that it is *inexpedient to inflict punishment*.

The discharge may be absolute or conditional. A conditional discharge may be for any period not exceeding three years. There is no minimum period.

It is not necessary for the offender to consent.

The following orders may be made in conjunction with a discharge: a compensation order, a confiscation order, a disqualification from driving, an order to pay prosecution costs, a recommendation for deportation, a banning order or an order under the Crime and Disorder Act 1998 s.1C (anti-social behaviour).

An offender who has been warned under the Crime and Disorder Act 1998 s.65 may not be conditionally discharged for an offence committed within two years of the warning, unless there are exceptional circumstances.

Conditional Discharge—Subsequent Conviction

P.C.C.(S.)A. 2000 s.13

References: Current Sentencing Practice D11–1; Archbold 5–170

The power to deal with an offender subject to a conditional discharge arises when he is convicted of an offence *committed during the period of the discharge,* whether or not the discharge is still effective when he appears before the court.

If the conditional discharge was granted by the Crown Court, the offender may be dealt with only by the Crown Court. A magistrates' court may commit the offender to the Crown Court to be dealt with in respect of the conditional discharge, and to be sentenced for the latest offence. (See **Committal for Sentence.**)

If the conditional discharge was granted by a magistrates' court, the offender may be dealt with either by the Crown Court or by a magistrates' court.

The court may deal with the offender as if he had just been convicted of the offence.

The offender should be sentenced on the basis of his current age, not his age on the date of conviction.

If the conditional discharge was granted by a magistrates' court, the court may deal with the offender for the offence in respect of which the conditional discharge was granted **in any way in which a magistrates' court could deal with him** for the offences concerned if it had just convicted him of that offence. *The Crown Court must observe the relevant limitations on the powers of the magistrates' court, in relation to maximum terms of imprisonment, aggregate terms of imprisonment, and financial penalties.*

If the offender is subject to two conditional discharges, the court may impose separate sentences for each of the offences in respect of which the orders were made.

If the court imposes a custodial sentence for the latest offence it will normally be appropriate for the court to impose a sentence for the original offence, which will terminate the conditional discharge, but there may be exceptional cases where it will be appropriate to leave the conditional discharge in effect.

Confiscation Order—Postponement of Proceedings

CRIMINAL JUSTICE ACT 1988 s.72A; DRUG TRAFFICKING ACT 1994 s.3, PROCEEDS OF CRIME ACT 2002 s.11

References: Current Sentencing Practice J10

Note: this section sets out a summary of decisions on postponement of confiscation proceedings under the Criminal Justice Act 1988 and the Drug Trafficking Act 1994. The statutory provisions governing postponement under the Proceeds of Crime Act 2002 are different from those under the two earlier Acts, but some of these decisions may apply to that Act.

All decisions on the postponement of confiscation orders must be considered in the light of the decision of the House of Lords in Soneji and Bullen [2006] 1 Cr.App.R.(S.) 79 (p.430).

The Crown Court must make the decision to proceed with a view to confiscation and to postpone the determination of the relevant matters, before sentencing the defendant.

A postponement of the determinations need not be for a specific period.

The decision to postpone is a judicial act, which must be performed in open court in the presence of both parties.

The decision to postpone requires the exercise of judicial discretion, which must be shown to be exercised.

If a court proposes to postpone inquiries for a period exceeding six months (two years where the Proceeds of Crime Act 2002 applies) from the date of conviction, it must identify "exceptional circumstances" for doing so and order the postponement before the end of the six-month period.

If the court properly postpones the determinations for a period which exceeds six months from the date of conviction on the grounds that there are "exceptional circumstances", it is not necessary for the court to find further exceptional circumstances for subsequent postponements.

The determination whether the circumstances which are relied on to justify a postponement beyond the period of six months from the date of conviction is a matter within the discretion of the sentencing judge, and the Court of Appeal, Criminal Division will not readily interfere with the judge's exercise of the discretion.

The period of six months beginning with the date of conviction includes the day on which the defendant is convicted itself.

A court which postpones the relevant determinations and proceeds to sentence the defendant before making a confiscation order should not impose a fine, make an order for the payment of prosecution costs, make an order under the Powers of Criminal Courts (Sentencing) Act 2000 s.143, or make an order under the Misuse of Drugs Act 1971 s.27(1), before making the confiscation order, but it may make a compensation order.

Confiscation Order—Proceeds of Crime Act 2002

PROCEEDS OF CRIME ACT 2002

References: Current Sentencing Practice J11–1; Archbold 5–785

The confiscation order provisions of the Proceeds of Crime Act 2002 apply only where all of the offences of which the offender has been convicted (but not those which he asks the court to take into consideration) were committed on or after March 24, 2003. *Where an offence has been committed over a period of two or more days, or at some time during a period of two or more days, it is taken to have been committed on the earliest of those days.*

To qualify for a confiscation order, the defendant must either have been:

convicted of an offence or offences in proceedings before the Crown Court;

committed to the Crown Court for sentence in respect of an offence or offences under the Powers of Criminal Courts (Sentencing) Act 2000 ss.3, 4 or 6;

or committed to the Crown Court under the Proceeds of Crime Act 2002 s.70.

If the defendant absconds after conviction, the Court may proceed under Proceeds of Crime Act 2002 s.27.

The court must proceed with a view to a confiscation order if it is asked to do so by the prosecutor, or if the court believes "it is appropriate for it to do so".

If the court believes that any victim of the offence has initiated, or intends to initiate, civil proceedings against the defendant, it is not bound to institute confiscation proceedings, but may do so in its discretion.

If the Crown Court embarks on confiscation proceedings, it must first decide whether the defendant has a **"criminal lifestyle"**.

A person has a "criminal lifestyle" if either:

he is convicted of one of the offences specified in Sch.2 of the Act; or

the offence constitutes "conduct forming part of a course of criminal activity"; or

if the offence was committed over a period of at least six months
and the defendant has benefited from the conduct.

An offence constitutes part of a course of criminal conduct if either:

the defendant has been convicted in the same proceedings of at least
four offences, he has benefited from at least four offences, and his
"relevant benefit" is at least £5,000; or

the defendant has been convicted on at least two separate occasions
during the period of six years ending with a day when the
proceedings for the present offence were started and has benefited
from the offences in respect of which he was convicted on both of
those occasions, and the "relevant benefit" amounts to at least
£5,000. The latest offence must have been committed on or after
March 24, 2003, but it is not necessary that the two earlier offences
should have been.

If the Court decides that the defendant has a **"criminal lifestyle"** it
must decide whether he has benefited from his **"general criminal
conduct"**. "General criminal conduct" is "all his criminal conduct", and it
is immaterial whether the conduct occurred before or after the passing of
this Act or whether property constituting a benefit from conduct was
obtained before or after the passing of the Act.

In making this decision, the Court **must** make any of the **assumptions**
required by s.10 which apply, *unless the assumption is "shown to be incorrect" or
there would be a "serious risk of injustice" if the assumption were made.*

The first assumption is that any property transferred to the defendant
within the period of six years ending on the day on which proceedings were
started against the defendant was obtained by him as a result of his
general criminal conduct.

The second assumption is that any property held by the defendant at any
time after the date of conviction was obtained by him as a result of his
general criminal conduct.

The third assumption is that any expenditure incurred by the defendant
within a period of six years ending with the date on which the proceedings
were started against him was met from property obtained by him as a
result of his general criminal conduct.

The fourth assumption is that any property obtained or assumed to have
been obtained by the defendant was free of any other interest in the
property.

If the court decides that the defendant **does not have a "criminal lifestyle"**, the court must then decide whether the defendant has benefited from his "**particular criminal conduct**". "Particular criminal conduct" is "all his criminal conduct" which "constitutes the offence or offences concerned", or "constitutes the offences of which he was convicted in the same proceedings as those in which he was convicted of the offence or offences concerned", or "constitutes offences which the court will be taking into consideration in deciding his sentence for the offence or offences concerned". **Benefit arising from offences committed before March 24, 2003, and which are taken into consideration, must be disregarded**.

Any question arising in connection with whether the defendant has a criminal life style or whether he has benefited from his general or particular criminal conduct must be decided on a "balance of probabilities".

The court must make an order for the amount which it has assessed to be the defendant's benefit, unless either:

> it believes that a victim of the offence has started or intends to start civil proceedings against the defendant (in which case the amount of the order is such amount "as the court believes is just", but the amount must not exceed the amount of the defendant's benefit;

> or the defendant shows that the "available amount" is less than the benefit (in which case the amount of the confiscation order is either the "available amount" itself, or a nominal amount).

The "**available amount**" includes the total of the values of all "free property" held by the defendant at the time the confiscation order is made, and the total value of all "**tainted gifts**".

If the Crown Court is proceeding with a view to a confiscation order on the application of the prosecutor, the prosecutor must give the Crown Court a statement of information. If the Crown Court is proceeding with a view to confiscation on its own initiative, it may order the prosecutor to give such a statement.

Where a statement of information has been given to the Court and a copy served on the defendant, the Crown Court may order the defendant to indicate to what extent he accepts the allegations made in the statement, and in so far as he does not accept an allegation, "to give particulars of any matters he proposes to rely on". If the defendant accepts any allegation, the Crown Court may treat that acceptance as conclusive. If the defendant fails to comply with an order, he may be treated as accepting every allegation in the statement of information other than an allegation in respect of which he has complied with the requirement, or an allegation that he has benefited from his general or particular criminal conduct.

No acceptance of an allegation by the defendant is admissible in evidence in proceedings for an offence.

The Crown Court may order the defendant to give it the "information specified in the order". There is no restriction on the kind of information which may be specified. If the defendant fails "without reasonable excuse" to comply with an order, the court "may draw such inference as it believes is appropriate" from the failure.

When the Crown Court makes a confiscation order it must make the following orders:

Appoint receiver (ss.50–55)

The Court may appoint an "enforcement receiver" on the application of the prosecutor.

Empower the receiver

The Court must confer on the enforcement receiver the powers under s.51

Transfer from management receiver to enforcement receiver (s.64)

Where a receiver has been appointed in connection with a restraint order, and the Crown Court makes a confiscation order and a receiver is appointed under s.50, the Crown Court must order the "management receiver" appointed in connection with the restraint order to transfer to the "enforcement receiver" appointed in connection with the confiscation order all property held by the first receiver by virtue of the exercise of his powers.

Allow time for payment (s.11)

If the defendant shows that he needs time to pay the order, **the court may make an order allowing payment to be made within a specified period** *which must not exceed six months* **from the day on which the confiscation order is made**.

If the defendant makes a further application to the Crown Court within the specified period and Court believes that there are "exceptional circumstances" it may make an order extending the period. *The extended period must not extend beyond 12 months from the day on which the confiscation order was made.*

Although the second application must be made within the original six-month specified period, the order extending the period may be made after the end of that period, but not after the end of the period of 12 months starting with the day on which the confiscation order was made.

It is not open to the Crown Court to make an order allowing 12 months for payment on the defendant's initial application, even though the defendant shows that there are exceptional circumstances in which this would be appropriate. The defendant must make a further application within the six-month period.

Fix term of imprisonment in default (ss.35, 36)

The Crown Court must fix a term of imprisonment to be served in default of the order, taking the terms from the table set out in the P.C.C.(S.)A. 2000 s.139(4); (See **Default Terms—Crown Court.**)

Sentencing the defendant for the offence (ss.13, 15, 71)

If the court postpones the confiscation proceedings under s.14, it may sentence the defendant in the normal way but must not make any of the orders specified in subs.(2). (These orders include a compensation order).

Where the defendant has been sentenced and subsequently a confiscation order is made following a postponement, the sentence originally passed may be varied by the addition of one of the orders mentioned in subs.(3) within 28 days starting with the last day of the period of postponement. This does not necessarily mean the day on which the confiscation order is actually made.

If the Crown Court makes a confiscation order before sentencing the defendant, the Crown Court when sentencing the defendant must take account of the confiscation order before imposing a fine, making any order involving payment by the defendant other than a compensation order, or making the other orders of forfeiture or deprivation specified in the section. *A court which has made a confiscation order may leave the confiscation order out of account in deciding whether to make a compensation order in favour of the victim of the offence and in deciding the amount of the order. It is open to the Crown Court to make a confiscation order and a compensation order in respect of the same offence, even though this means that the defendant will be required to pay twice the amount involved in the offence.*

In deciding the appropriate sentence for the offence, where it is not a financial penalty, the confiscation order must be left out of account. *The defendant cannot claim that his sentence should be mitigated because a confiscation order has been made.*

If the defendant has been committed for sentence under s.70 for an either way offence, the powers of the Crown Court to deal with the offender for the offence depend on whether the magistrates' court at the time of committal stated in accordance with s.70(5) that it would have committed the defendant for sentence under the P.C.C.(S.)A. 2000 s.3. If it did, the Crown Court must inquire into the circumstances of the case and may deal with the defendant in any way in which it could deal with him if he had just been convicted of the offence on indictment. If the magistrates' court did not make a statement under s.70(5) in respect of an either way offence, or the offence is not an either way offence, the Crown Court, having inquired into the circumstances of the case, may deal with the defendant in any way in which the magistrates' court could deal with him if it had just convicted him of the offence.

Enforcing the default term (ss.35–39)

All questions relating to serving the default term will be dealt with in the magistrates' court, in the same way as a fine, subject to the amendments made by s.35(3) to the normal procedure.

Consecutive Sentences

CRIMINAL JUSTICE ACT 2003 s.265

References: Current Sentencing Practice A5–1; Archbold 5–585, 5–668

Consecutive sentences of imprisonment should not normally be passed in respect of offences which arise out of the same transaction or incident, but may be passed in exceptional circumstances in such cases.

Consecutive sentences should normally be passed in the following cases:

(a) where a burglar uses violence towards an occupant of premises who interrupts him;

(b) where violence is used to resist arrest for the primary offence;

(c) where an offender is convicted of an offence under the Firearms Act 1968 committed by having a firearm with him at the time of another offence;

(d) where one offence is committed while the offender is on bail in connection with the other offence;

(e) where a community order is revoked following the offender's conviction of a further offence;

(f) where a suspended sentence is activated following the offender's conviction of a further offence;

(g) where an offender is convicted of doing an act tending to pervert the course of justice in relation to the other offence.

In all cases, whether or not the sentences are passed on the same occasion or by the same sentencer, the court should have regard to the principle of totality and review the aggregate sentence to ensure that it is just and appropriate for the offender's behaviour, taken as a whole.

A sentence of life imprisonment should not be imposed to run consecutively to any other sentence, and no sentence may be ordered to run consecutively to a sentence of life imprisonment. If a court imposes such a sentence in circumstances in which the sentence would normally be consecutive to another sentence, it should make an appropriate adjustment to the minimum term. (See **Minimum Term.**) If an offender who is serving the minimum term of an indeterminate sentence falls to be sentenced for another offence, the court may impose a determinate sentence to begin at the expiry of the minimum term of the indeterminate sentence.

A court must not order a term of imprisonment to commence on the expiration of any other sentence of imprisonment from which the offender has already been released and in respect of which his licence has been revoked.

Criminal Behaviour Orders

Anti-social Behaviour, Crime and Policing Act 2014 s.22

General

Note: These orders were brought into force on October 20, 2014 and apply to proceedings commenced after that date: ASBCPA 2014 s.33(1)(b). For proceedings commenced before that date, see Anti-Social Behaviour Order on Conviction.

Purpose: Statutory guidance issued by the Home Office states that the order is aimed at tackling the most serious and persistent offenders where their anti-social behaviour has brought them before a criminal court.

Availability: The power to make a CBO is available where a person is convicted of an offence and where the court imposes a sentence or conditional discharge: ASBCPA 2014 s.22(1) and (6).

For offenders aged under 18 when the application is made, the prosecution must find out the views of the local youth offending team before applying: ASBCPA 2014 s.22(8).

Test: The court must be satisfied beyond reasonable doubt that:

(a) the offender has engaged in behaviour that caused or was likely to cause harassment, alarm or distress to any person; and

(b) making the order will help in preventing the offender from engaging in such behaviour. (ASBCPA 2014 s.22(3) and (4).)

Note: this is a lower test than the test for imposing a post-conviction ASBO.

Prosecution must apply: An order may only be made on the application of the prosecution: ASBCPA 2014 s.22(7).

How long may the order last/When does it take effect?

Effective date: The order takes effect on the day it is made, save for where on the day an order is made the offender is subject to another criminal behaviour order. In such a circumstance, the new order may be made so as to take effect on the day on which the previous order ceases to have effect: ASBCPA 2014 s.25(1) and (2).

Length—aged 18+ when order made: either a fixed period of not more than two years, or for an indefinite period: ASBCPA 2014 s.25(4).

Length—aged under 18 when order made: a fixed period of not less than one year and not more than three years: ASBCPA 2014 s.25(4).

Prohibitions and requirements forming part of the order

Contents: The order may, for the purpose of preventing the offender from engaging in such behaviour, prohibit the offender from doing anything, or require the offender to do anything, described in the order.

The order may specify periods for which particular prohibitions or requirements have effect: ASBCPA 2014 s.25(6).

Must hear from supervising officer: Before including a requirement, the court must receive evidence about its suitability and enforceability from the supervising officer: ASBCPA 2014 s.24(1) and (2).

Suitability of prohibitions and requirements: Prohibitions and requirements must avoid any interference with the times at which the offender normally works or attends an educational establishment and any conflict with the requirements of any other court order or injunction to which the offender may be subject: ASBCPA 2014 s.22(9).

Obligations on the offender: An offender must keep in touch with the person responsible for supervising compliance in relation to a requirement and notify the person of any change of address. These obligations have effect as requirements of the order: ASBCPA 2014 s.24(6).

Review periods

A CBO is subject to review periods every 12 months, beginning on the day on which the order took effect, or the day on which it was varied or most recently varied: ASBCPA 2014 s.28(2).

Content of review: A review must consider:

(a) the extent to which the offender has complied with the order;

(b) the adequacy of any support available to the offender to help him or her comply with it;

(c) any matters relevant to the question whether an application should be made for the order to be varied or discharged, ASBCPA 2014 s.28(3).

Interim orders

The court may make a criminal behaviour order that lasts until the final hearing of the application or until further order if the court thinks it just to do so: ASBCPA 2014 s.26(2).

There is no requirement to consult the local youth offending team, that the prosecution make an application, or that the order is in addition to a sentence or conditional discharge: ASBCPA 2014 s.26(3).

The court has the same powers whether or not the criminal behaviour order is an interim order.

Variation and discharge

Power: An order may be varied or discharged by the court which made it on the application of the offender, or the prosecution: ASBCPA 2014 s.27(1).

Extent of power: The power to vary an order includes power to include an additional prohibition or requirement in the order or to extend the period for which a prohibition or requirement has effect: ASBCPA 2014, s.27(4).

Bar on future applications: If an application by the offender is dismissed, the offender may make no further application without the consent of the court which made the order, or the agreement of the prosecution: ASBCPA 2014 s.27(2).

If an application by the prosecution is dismissed, the prosecution may make no further application without the consent of the court which made the order, or the agreement of the offender: ASBCPA 2014 s.27(3).

Breach

Offence: A person who, without reasonable excuse, does anything prohibited or fails to do anything required by a criminal behaviour order, commits an offence: ASBCPA 2014 s.30(1).

Maximum sentence: five years: ASBCPA 2014 s.30(2).

Conditional discharge: A court may not impose a conditional discharge for a breach of a CBO: ASBCPA 2014 s.30(3).

Reporting restrictions: YJCEA 1999 s.45 (power to restrict reporting of criminal proceedings involving persons under 18) applies to proceedings for a breach of a CBO, but CYPA 1933 s.49 does not apply: ASBCPA 2014 s.30(5).

Custodial Sentences—Criminal Justice Act 2003— General Criteria

CRIMINAL JUSTICE ACT 2003 ss.152, 153, 156

References: Current Sentencing Practice A2A; Archbold 5–458

A court must not pass a custodial sentence unless it is of the opinion that the offence or the combination of the offence and one or more offences associated with it **was so serious that neither a fine alone nor a community sentence can be justified for the offence**.

This requirement does not apply to sentences fixed by law, mandatory or required minimum sentences under the P.C.C.(S.)A. 2000 ss.110 and 111, the Firearms Act 1968 s.51A, the Prevention of Crime Act 1953 s.1A(5), the Violent Crime Reduction Act 2006 s.29 or the Criminal Justice Act 1988 s.139AA(7), or sentences of life imprisonment or detention under ss.224A, 225 or 226.

It is not a justification for a discretionary custodial sentence that the offence is a sexual or violent offence and only a custodial sentence would be adequate to protect the public from serious harm from the offender.

A custodial sentence may be passed for an offence which is not "so serious that neither a fine alone nor a community sentence can be justified" if the offender refuses to express his willingness to comply with a proposed requirement of a community order which requires him to express his willingness to comply. *The relevant requirements are a mental health treatment requirement, a drug rehabilitation requirement, and an alcohol treatment requirement.* It is not necessary for the offender to express his willingness to comply with an unpaid work requirement.

Length of discretionary custodial sentences

Subject to a required minimum sentence under:

(i) the PCC(S)A 2000 ss.110 or 111,

(ii) the Firearms Act 1968 s.51A,

(iii) the Prevention of Crime Act 1953 s.1A(5),

(iv) the Violent Crime Reduction Act 2006 s.29

(v) the Criminal Justice Act 1988 s.139AA(7), or

(vi) an extended sentence under CJA 2003 s.226A or 226B,

a custodial sentence must be for the **shortest term (not exceeding the permitted maximum) that in the opinion of the court is commensurate with the seriousness of the offence**, or the combination of the offence and one or more offences associated with it.

Information

The court must take account of all available information about the circumstances of the offence when forming an opinion about the seriousness of the offence, for the purpose of deciding whether the offence is so serious that a custodial sentence is necessary and what is the shortest term which is commensurate with the seriousness of the offence.

Reports

If a court proposes to impose a custodial sentence on an offender over the age of 18 on any ground other than the failure of an offender to express his willingness to comply with one of the orders mentioned in s.152(3) it must "obtain and consider" a pre-sentence report unless it is of the opinion "that it is unnecessary" to do so.

In the case of an offender under the age of 18, a pre-sentence report is mandatory before the court imposes a custodial sentence (other than on the basis of a failure to express willingness under s.152 (3). (*The exception in the P.C.C.(S.)A. 2000 s.81 for cases where one of the offences for which the offender is to be sentenced is triable only on indictment is not repeated in this provision*).

If the sentencing court does not obtain a pre-sentence report, where such a report is required, the failure does not affect the validity of the sentence or order of the court, but any appellate court dealing with the case is placed under similar obligations, subject to the same exceptions.

Custody for Life

P.C.C.(S.)A. 2000 ss.93, 94

References: Current Sentencing Practice E3; Archbold 5—614

Where a person aged under 21 is convicted of murder, he must be sentenced to custody for life unless he is liable to be detained during Her Majesty's pleasure (see **Murder**).

Where a person aged 18 and under 21 on the date of conviction satisfies the requirements of the Criminal Justice Act 2003 s. 225(1) (see **Specified Offences—Adult Offenders**) the court must impose a sentence of custody for life.

Where a person aged 18 and under 21 on the date of conviction is convicted of an offence punishable with imprisonment for life committed before April 4, 2005, the court may impose a sentence of custody for life in appropriate circumstances.

A court which imposes a sentence of custody for life must fix a minimum term in accordance with the relevant provisions (see **Minimum Term** and **Murder**).

Default Terms (Crown Court)

P.C.C.(S.)A. 2000 s.139

References: Current Sentencing Practice J1–1A01; Archbold 5–676

If the Crown Court imposes a fine or makes a confiscation order, the court must fix a term of imprisonment in default of payment of the fine.

The following table shows the default terms applicable to fines and confiscation orders.

Fine	Term
Not exceeding £200	7 days
More than £200, not exceeding £500	14 days
More than £500, not exceeding £1,000	28 days
More than £1,000, not exceeding £2,500	45 days
More than £2,500, not exceeding £5,000	3 months
More than £5,000, not exceeding £10,000	6 months
More than £10,000, not exceeding £20,000	12 months
More than £20,000, not exceeding £50,000	18 months
More than £50,000, not exceeding £100,000	2 years
More than £100,000, not exceeding £250,000	3 years
More than £250,000, not exceeding £1 million	5 years
Over £1 million	10 years

These terms are maximum terms for the sums in question; the court should exercise its discretion and fix an appropriate default term within the relevant maximum. The court may also allow time for payment and may fix instalments.

The Crown Court does not fix a default term when it makes a compensation order or orders the offender to pay the costs of the prosecution, but may enlarge the powers of the magistrates' court.

Deferment of Sentence

P.C.C.(S.)A. 2000 ss.1, 2

References: Current Sentencing Practice L8; Archbold 5–45

These provisions apply to all offences irrespective of the date on which the offence was committed.

Either the magistrates' court or the Crown Court may defer passing sentence on an offender for the purpose of enabling the court to have regard to his conduct after conviction (including the making by him of reparation for the offence) or any change to his circumstances.

The power may be exercised only if the offender **consents** and **undertakes to comply with any requirements** as to his conduct during the period of deferment that the court considers it appropriate to impose. *The court is not obliged to impose requirements on deferring sentence.* The court must also be satisfied that it would be in the interests of justice to defer sentence.

Sentence may be deferred for a period of **not more than six months**.

The requirements which the court may require the offender to comply with during the period of deferment are not specified, but it is provided that a residence requirement may be imposed and that the court may appoint an officer of a local probation board or other person to act as a supervisor. *The statutory power is not limited to the requirements which may be imposed in connection with a community order.* If the offender fails to comply with the requirements imposed during the period of deferment, he may be brought before the court and dealt with before the end of the period of deferment.

A court which has deferred sentence may deal with the offender before the end of the period of deferment if he is convicted of an offence during the deferment period. If the conviction for the later offence occurs in England and Wales, the court which sentences him for the later offence may deal with him for the offence or offences in respect of which sentence has been deferred, but a magistrates' court may not deal with an offender in respect of a sentence deferred by the Crown Court, and if the Crown Court deals with an offender in respect of a sentence deferred by a magistrates' court, the Crown Court may not pass a sentence which could not have been passed by a magistrates' court.

Deprivation Order

P.C.C.(S.)A. 2000 s.143

References: Current Sentencing Practice J4–1; Archbold 5–726

A court may order an offender to be deprived of his rights in property **which has been used, or was intended to be used, to commit or facilitate the commission of an offence, or in property of which he was unlawfully in possession**.

The power may be used in addition to any other sentence for the offence, or as the only sentence for the offence.

The power may be used by the Crown Court or by a magistrates' court on conviction for any offence.

The court must be satisfied that either:

(a) the property has been used for the purpose of committing or facilitating the commission of any offence; or

(b) the property was intended by the offender to be used for the purpose of committing or facilitating the commission of any offence; or

(c) that the offender has been convicted of unlawful possession of the property concerned; or

(d) that an offence of unlawfully possessing the property concerned has been taken into consideration.

The property must either:

(a) *have been lawfully seized from the offender; or*

(b) *have been in his possession or control at the time when he was apprehended for the offence; or*

(c) *have been in his possession or control at the time when a summons in respect of the offence was issued.*

"Facilitating the commission of an offence" includes *"the taking of any steps after it has been committed for the purpose of disposing of any property to which it relates or of avoiding apprehension or detection"*.

It is not necessary that the offence in relation to which the property has been used or was intended to be used should be the offence of which the offender has been convicted.

If a person commits an offence under the Road Traffic Act 1988 punishable with imprisonment, manslaughter, or wanton and furious driving contrary to Offences against the Person Act 1861 s.35 by driving, attempting to drive or being in charge of a vehicle, failing to provide a specimen for analysis or laboratory test, or failing to stop and give information or report an accident, the vehicle shall be regarded as used for the purpose of committing the offence and any offence of aiding the commission of the offence.

The power to make a deprivation order may not be used in relation to property taken from the offender, which has been used by another person to commit an offence.

Deprivation orders do not apply to land or buildings.

A deprivation order should not be made without a proper investigation of the grounds for making an order. A court considering whether to make an order under the section must have regard to the value of the property and must normally have evidence of the value of the property concerned before making a deprivation order.

A court considering whether to make a deprivation order must have regard to the likely financial and other effects on the offender of the order, taken together with any other order that the court contemplates making.

A deprivation order should be considered as part of the total sentence, and the court should bear in mind that the overall penalty, including the deprivation order, should be commensurate with the offence.

Where a deprivation order is to be made against one of a number of offenders, who are all equally responsible, there may be unjustifiable disparity.

A court which has made a deprivation order may order the proceeds arising from the sale of the property, not exceeding a figure specified by the court, to be paid to a person who has suffered loss, damage or personal injury as a result of the offence of which the offender has been convicted, or which he has asked the court to take into consideration, if the court would have made a compensation order in favour of the victim but was prevented from doing so by the inadequacy of the offender's means.

Where a court has postponed confiscation proceedings and proceeds to sentence the offender before making the confiscation order, it must not make a deprivation order until the confiscation order has been made.

Detention under Powers of Criminal Courts (Sentencing) Act 2000 s.91

P.C.C.(S.)A. 2000 s.91

References: Current Sentencing Practice E4–1; Archbold 5–610

The power to award detention under the P.C.C.(S.)A. 2000 s.91, applies to:

(a) offenders aged at least 10 and under 18 who are convicted on indictment of any offence punishable in the case of an adult with imprisonment for 14 years or more (other than an offence the sentence for which is fixed by law), or an offence under ss.3, 13, 25 or 26 of the Sexual Offences Act 2003.

(b) offenders aged between 16 and 18 convicted of certain offences contrary to the Firearms Act 1968 s.5.

(c) offenders between the ages of 16 and 18 convicted of an offence under the Violent Crime Reduction Act 2006 s.28, involving a weapon to which the Firearms Act 1968 s.5, applies (with certain exceptions), unless there are exceptional circumstances.

A sentence of detention under the P.C.C.(S.)A. 2000 s.91 is a custodial sentence and may be imposed only if the general requirements for a custodial sentence are satisfied. (See **Custodial Sentences—Criminal Justice Act 2003— General Criteria.**)

The power may be exercised only if the court is of the opinion that *neither a youth rehabilitation order nor a detention and training order is suitable.*

Where the power is available, the court may sentence the offender to be detained for such period not exceeding the maximum term of imprisonment for the offence as the court specifies. **There is no statutory minimum period**. A sentence of detention for life may be passed in an appropriate case. A sentence of detention for less than two years may be passed in appropriate circumstances.

Where the offender is to be sentenced for a number of associated offences, the court may pass a single sentence of detention which is commensurate with the seriousness of all the associated offences (including those for which detention under s.91 is not available) and impose no separate penalty for the other offences, provided that the other offences do not attract mandatory sentences.

The power may be exercised only where the offender is convicted on indictment.

An offender sentenced to detention under the P.C.C.(S.)A. 2000 s.91 is subject to the same provisions relating to early release as one sentenced to imprisonment.

Detention and Training Order

P.C.C.(S.)A. 2000 ss.100–107

References: Current Sentencing Practice E1–1; Archbold 5–597

A detention and training order may be made in the case of a child or young person convicted of an offence punishable with imprisonment.

A detention and training order is a custodial sentence and the criteria for the imposition of a custodial sentence must be satisfied. (See **Custodial Sentences—Criminal Justice Act 2003—General Criteria.**)

If the offender is **under 15**, in addition the court must be of the opinion that the offender is a "**persistent offender**".

If the offender is **under 12**, in addition the court must be of the opinion that only a custodial sentence would be adequate to protect the public from further offending by the offender and the offence must have been committed on or after the appointed day. *No day had been appointed for this purpose by December 1, 2012.*

These conditions are cumulative.

The maximum term of a detention and training order is two years, or whatever sentence the Crown Court might impose for the offence, if less. The powers of the youth court to impose detention and training orders are not restricted to those of a magistrates' court. Any period in excess of 24 months is automatically remitted.

A detention and training order must be for 4, 6, 8, 10, 12, 18 or 24 months. No other period may be specified.

In determining the length of a detention and training order, the court must take account of any period for which the offender has been remanded in custody or on bail subject to a qualifying curfew condition in connection with the offence. This includes time spent in police detention and in local authority secure accommodation. **Time in custody on remand is not deducted automatically.** The court must also make such allowance as is appropriate for a plea of guilty.

If the offender is convicted of more than one offence, or is convicted of offences while he is subject to an existing detention and training order, the court may pass consecutive detention and training orders, so long as the aggregate of the orders to which the offender is subject does not exceed two years. *The court may impose consecutive detention and training orders which amount in aggregate to a term which would not be lawful as a single detention and training order.*

A detention and training order may be ordered to run consecutively to a term of detention under the Powers of Criminal Courts (Sentencing) Act 2000 s.91 or an extended sentence of detention.

Offence committed after release

If an offender who has been released from a detention and training order commits an offence punishable with imprisonment during the period between his release and the end of the term of the order, the court which sentences him for that offence may order him to be detained for the whole or any part of a period equivalent to the period which remained of the original order on the date the offence was committed.

The period of detention must begin on the date when the order is made. Any sentence imposed for the new offence may run concurrently with the order for detention or consecutively to it, but the order for detention must not be ordered to run consecutively to any other sentence.

Where a court makes a further detention and training order in respect of an offender who has been sentenced to a detention and training order from which he has been released, the length of the original detention and training order is disregarded for the purposes of the two year aggregate limit. It is uncertain whether a period of renewed detention counts against the aggregate for this purpose.

Breach of supervision requirement

If an offender fails to comply with a supervision requirement, he may be brought before the appropriate youth court who may order him to be detained for a period not exceeding the remainder of the order or three months, whichever is the less.

Detention in a Young Offender Institution

P.C.C.(S.)A. 2000 s.96

References: Current Sentencing Practice E2–1; Archbold 5–594

Note: the sentence of detention in a young offender institution is abolished by Criminal Justice and Court Services Act 2000 s.61 with effect from a day to be appointed. No day had been appointed by December 3, 2012. The minimum age for imprisonment is reduced by the same Act to 18 (see Sch.7, para.180). That provision had not been brought into force on December 3, 2012. References in the Criminal Justice Act 2003 to sentences of imprisonment are for the most part to be read as references to imprisonment or detention in a young offender institution.

A sentence of detention in a young offender institution may be passed on an offender aged 18 and under 21 on the day of conviction.

The sentence is a custodial sentence and the general requirements for custodial sentences apply. (See **Custodial Sentences—Criminal Justice Act 2003—General Criteria.**)

The minimum term of a sentence of detention in a young offender institution is 21 days. The maximum term is the maximum term of imprisonment available to the court for the offence.

The sentence takes effect in the same way as a sentence of imprisonment.

A sentence of detention in a young offender institution passed for an offence committed on or after April 4, 2005, may be subject to a suspended sentence order. (See **Suspended Sentence Order.**)

Detention in Default or for Contempt

P.C.C.(S.)A. 2000 s.108

References: Current Sentencing Practice E9; Archbold 5—1296

In any case where a court would have power to commit a person aged at least 18 and under 21 to prison in default of payment of a fine or other sum of money, or for contempt, the court may commit the person to be detained for a term not exceeding the appropriate term of imprisonment. *The court may not commit a person to be detained unless it is of the opinion that no other method of dealing with him is appropriate*, and in forming that opinion the court must take into account all such information about the default or contempt as is available to it and may take into account any information about the person which is before it.

If a magistrates' court commits a person to be detained, it must state in open court the reason for its opinion that no other method of dealing with him is appropriate and cause that reason to be specified in the warrant of commitment.

Discount for Guilty Plea

CRIMINAL JUSTICE ACT 2003 s.144

References: Current Sentencing Practice A8–1; Archbold 5–107

Sentencing Guidelines Council Definitive Guideline: Reduction in Sentence for a Guilty Plea (Revised 2007).

As a general rule, a court which imposes a custodial sentence should reduce the length of the sentence to recognise the fact that the offender has pleaded guilty. The extent of the reduction is a matter for the discretion of the court.

It will not normally be appropriate to impose the maximum sentence for an offence on an offender who has pleaded guilty, unless there are grounds for refusing any discount.

A discount may be refused or reduced if the protection of the public requires a long sentence, or the offender has withheld his plea until a late stage in the case. A discount may be reduced if the defendant has unsuccessfully contested a Newton hearing. (See **Newton Hearings.**)

A court which passes a custodial sentence following a plea of guilty should always indicate that it has taken the plea into account.

There is a statutory duty in all cases to take into account the stage in the proceedings for the offence at which the offender indicated his intention to plead guilty, and the circumstances in which this indication was given.

Disparity of Sentence

References: Current Sentencing Practice A9–2; Archbold 5–154

As a general rule, when two or more offenders are convicted of the same offence, and their individual responsibility is the same, and there is no relevant difference in their personal circumstances, they should receive the same sentence.

There is no disparity if a difference in sentence reflects a difference in the respective responsibilities of the offenders, or a difference in their ages, previous convictions, or the existence of personal mitigating factors peculiar to one of them. Where one offender has the benefit of personal mitigation which is not available to other offenders, the other offenders should not be given the benefit of that mitigation.

There is no disparity if one offender who is likely to respond favourably to a community order is dealt with by means of a community order and the other offender is not.

A difference in sex is not in itself a reason for discriminating between offenders.

There may be objectionable disparity if one offender receives a more severe sentence than a co-defendant, and there are no relevant differences in their responsibility or personal mitigation; where two offenders receive the same sentence, despite a difference in their responsibility or personal mitigation; or where the difference in their sentences is either too large or too small to reflect the difference in their responsibility or personal mitigation.

There is no disparity where one offender has received an appropriate sentence and his co-defendant has received a lesser sentence as a result of statutory restrictions which apply only to him, or where an accomplice has been sentenced in a foreign jurisdiction where sentencing laws and practices are different from those of England and Wales.

There is no disparity where one offender who qualifies for a longer than commensurate sentence receives such a sentence, and a co-defendant who does not qualify does not receive one.

Where an offender has already been sentenced by one judge, another judge who on a later occasion has to deal with his accomplice should pass the sentence on the accomplice which he considers appropriate, without regard to the sentence passed on the other offender.

Where there is an unjustified disparity in the sentences passed on two offenders, the Court of Appeal may reduce the more severe sentence if the disparity is so substantial as to create the appearance of injustice.

Disqualification from Directing Company

COMPANY DIRECTORS DISQUALIFICATION ACT 1986 s.2

References: Current Sentencing Practice H5–1; Archbold 5–1116

Indictable offences: The court may make a disqualification order where a person is convicted of an indictable offence (whether on indictment or summarily) in connection with the promotion, formation, management, liquidation or striking off of a company with the receivership of a company's property or with his being an administrative receiver of a company: CDDA 1986 s.2(1).

Summary offences: Where a person is convicted of a summary offence, in consequence of a contravention of, or failure to comply with, any provision of the companies legislation requiring a return, account or other document to be filed with, delivered or sent, or notice of any matter to be given, to the registrar of companies (whether the contravention or failure is on the person's own part or on the part of any company) and during the five years ending with the date of the conviction, the person has had made against him, or has been convicted of, in total not less than three default orders and offences as specified above, the court may make a disqualification order: CDDA 1986 s.5(1)–(3).

The offence concerned may relate to the internal management of the company, or the general conduct of its business.

It is not necessary in a criminal case for the court to consider the tests of fitness required for the purposes of an order under s.6 of the Act.

The period of a disqualification order is determined by the court in the exercise of its discretion. The maximum term is 15 years (where the order is made by a magistrates' court, five years). There is no minimum period.

If the offender is already subject to a disqualification order, any new order will run concurrently with the existing order.

The court should inform counsel of its intentions and invite him to mitigate on the question before making an order of disqualification.

Disqualification from Driving—Discretionary

ROAD TRAFFIC OFFENDERS ACT 1988 s.34

References: Current Sentencing Practice H1–1; Archbold 32–168

The following offences are subject to discretionary disqualification but not endorsement:

(a) stealing or attempting to steal a motor vehicle;

(b) taking a motor vehicle without consent, or being carried;

(c) going equipped to steal a motor vehicle.

If an offender is convicted of any of these offences, the court may order the offender to be disqualified for such period as it thinks fit. There is no maximum or minimum period.

Most offences which are subject to obligatory endorsement, are also subject to discretionary disqualification. See Road Traffic Offenders Act 1988 Sch.2. The same principles apply in these cases.

If the court proposes to disqualify, the offender's advocate should be warned of the possibility of disqualification.

There is no obligation to disqualify. If the court does disqualify, the court does not award penalty points.

Disqualification from Driving—General Power

P.C.C.(S.)A. 2000 s.146

References: Current Sentencing Practice H3A–1; Archbold 5–1106

Any court may disqualify an offender from driving on conviction for any offence, either in addition to any other sentence or instead of any other sentence.

If the sentence for the offence is fixed by law, or the court is required to impose a mandatory custodial sentence, the court may impose a disqualification in addition to the sentence.

The power to disqualify may be used by the Crown Court or a magistrates' court.

It is not necessary that the offence should be connected in any way with the use of a motor vehicle.

The power may be used in respect of an offender who does not hold a driving licence.

Disqualification from Driving—Obligatory

ROAD TRAFFIC OFFENDERS ACT 1988 s.34

References: Current Sentencing Practice H1–1; Archbold 32–168

The following offences are subject to obligatory disqualification:

(a) causing death by dangerous driving;

(b) causing serious injury by dangerous driving;

(c) dangerous driving;

(d) causing death by careless driving while under the influence of drink or drugs;

(e) causing death by careless or inconsiderate driving;

(f) causing death by driving while unlicensed, disqualified or uninsured;

(g) driving or attempting to drive while unfit;

(h) driving or attempting to drive with excess alcohol;

(i) failing to provide a specimen for analysis (driving or attempting to drive);

(j) failing to allow a specimen to be subject to a laboratory test (driving or attempting to drive);

(k) racing or speed trials;

(l) manslaughter;

(m) aggravated vehicle taking;

(n) using vehicle in dangerous condition within three years of previous conviction for same offence.

The court **must disqualify unless there are special reasons for not disqualifying**, or for disqualifying for a shorter period. The obligation to establish special reasons lies on the defendant.

The existence of special reasons must be established by the defendant by calling evidence on the relevant matter, unless the prosecution are willing to admit the existence of the facts which are alleged to constitute special reasons. The defendant must establish the relevant facts on the balance of probabilities.

A special reason is an extenuating circumstance directly relating to the circumstances of the offence. Matters related to the effect of disqualification on the offender, or his employer or clients or patients, cannot constitute special reasons for this purpose.

The following matters have been held to be capable of amounting to special reasons in excess alcohol cases:

(a) the fact that the defendant consumed alcohol in the expectation that he would not be required to drive again that day, but was required to drive as a result of a sudden emergency;

(b) the fact that the defendant's consumption of excess alcohol was due to the act of another person who had laced his drink, or caused him to drink stronger liquor than he thought he was drinking;

(c) the fact that the defendant has driven an extremely short distance in circumstances where there was no risk to other road users.

Each of these matters may amount to a special reason in narrowly defined circumstances.

The following matters have been held not to be capable of amounting to special reasons:

(a) the fact that the defendant's alcohol level is only just over the relevant limit;

(b) the fact that the defendant's capacity to drive was not affected;

(c) the fact the defendant's peculiar metabolism caused him to retain the alcohol in his body for longer than the normal period;

(d) the fact that no other road user was endangered by the defendant's driving;

(e) the fact that the defendant had lost or destroyed part of his sample;

(f) the fact that the defendant had taken a test earlier on the same day which proved negative;

(g) the fact that the defendant had consumed the alcohol the day before he was tested and assumed that he had slept it off overnight.

If the court finds that special reasons exist, **it is not obliged to disqualify the defendant, but may do so in the exercise of its discretion**. Before disqualifying, where disqualification is discretionary, the court should inform counsel of its intention and invite submissions on the question of disqualification.

If the court finds that special reasons exist and does not disqualify, the court must award penalty points (within the range of 3 to 11) and follow the penalty points procedure. (See Disqualification from Driving—Penalty Points).

If the court finds no special reasons, it must disqualify for at least 12 months, unless either:

(a) the defendant is convicted of manslaughter, causing death by dangerous driving, or causing death by careless driving while under the influence of drink or drugs—minimum two years; or

(b) the defendant has been twice disqualified for 56 days or more in the three years before the commission of the present offence— minimum two years; or

(c) the defendant has been convicted of an excess alcohol offence and has been convicted of an excess alcohol offence within the last 10 years—minimum three years; or

(d) the defendant has been convicted of using a vehicle in a dangerous condition within three years of a conviction for a similar offence— six months.

The court may disqualify the offender for any period longer than the minimum.

If the defendant is convicted of manslaughter, causing death by dangerous driving, causing death by careless driving when affected by alcohol, committed on or after January 31, 2002 or dangerous driving, **the court must order him to take an extended driving test.** *This does not apply to a defendant convicted of causing death by careless driving contrary to Road Traffic Act 1988 s.2B.*

If the defendant is convicted of any other offence involving obligatory disqualification the court may order him to take a further driving test.

If the court disqualifies the defendant, it does not award penalty points.

Disqualification from Driving—Penalty Points

ROAD TRAFFIC OFFENDERS ACT 1988 s.35

References: Current Sentencing Practice H2–1; Archbold 32–168

If the offender is convicted of an offence subject to obligatory endorsement, the court must determine the number of penalty points which are to be attributed to the offence from the table below. If the table shows a range of points, the court must determine a number within that range.

(For offences not shown below, see Road Traffic Offenders Act 1988 Sch.2.)

Offence	Penalty
Speeding	3–6
Careless driving	3–9
Being in charge of vehicle when unfit to drive	10
Being in charge of vehicle with excess alcohol level	10
Failing to provide breath specimen	4
Failing to provide specimen when disqualification not obligatory	10
Leaving vehicle in dangerous position	3
Failing to comply with directions or signs	3
Using vehicle in dangerous condition	3
Driving without licence	3
Driving with uncorrected eyesight	3
Driving while disqualified	6
Using vehicle without insurance	6–8
Failing to stop after accident	5–10
Failing to give information as to driver	6

(*if committed on or after September 24, 2007; otherwise 3*).

If the offender has committed more than one offence on the same occasion, the court must normally determine points only for the offence carrying the highest number of points, unless the court decides to determine points for other offences.

The court must add to these penalty points any other points on the offender's licence, except points for offences committed more than three years before the date of the commission of the offences for which points have just been awarded and points awarded before a disqualification imposed on the basis of penalty points.

If the total number of points is 12 or more, the defendant must be disqualified, unless there are grounds for mitigating the normal consequences of conviction.

The defendant must establish the mitigating grounds, normally by calling evidence.

The following matters may not constitute grounds for mitigating the normal consequences of conviction:

(a) circumstances alleged to make the offence or any of the offences not a serious one;

(b) hardship, other than exceptional hardship;

(c) any circumstances which have been taken into account as mitigating grounds within the last three years.

The fact that the offender has been sentenced to custody on this occasion may constitute a mitigating ground in an appropriate case.

If the court finds that there are mitigating grounds, the court may either disqualify for a shorter period than would otherwise be required, or refrain from disqualifying at all.

If the court does not disqualify, it should order the licence to be endorsed with the appropriate penalty points unless there are special reasons for not doing so. The offender may be ordered to take a further driving test.

If the defendant does not establish mitigating grounds, the court must disqualify him for at least the relevant minimum period; there is no maximum period.

The normal minimum period is six months. If there are previous disqualifications to be taken into account, the minimum period of disqualification may be 12 months or two years. The court may order the offender to take an extended driving test.

If the offender has been convicted of manslaughter, causing death by dangerous driving, or dangerous driving, and has been disqualified for a period less than the normal statutory minimum, the court must order him to take an extended driving test.

Disqualification from Driving—Vehicle used for Crime

P.C.C.(S.)A. 2000 s.147

References: Current Sentencing Practice H3–1; Archbold 5–1107

The power to disqualify from driving where a vehicle has been used in connection with the commission of a crime may be exercised by the Crown Court where the offender has been convicted of any offence punishable with at least two years' imprisonment.

The power may be exercised by the Crown Court or by a magistrates' court where the offence consists of an assault committed by driving a vehicle.

The offender or an accomplice must have used the motor vehicle for the purpose of committing or facilitating the commission of the offence of which the offender has been convicted. This includes taking any steps after the offence has been committed to dispose of any property to which the offence relates, or to avoid apprehension or detection. It is not necessary that the offender should have been carried in the vehicle himself, or have driven the vehicle himself.

The power to disqualify may not be exercised on a conviction for conspiracy, if the only use of the vehicle is in the course of carrying out the conspiracy.

The court should inform counsel for the offender of its intentions and invite him to address the court on the question of disqualification.

The court should not impose a disqualification from driving if its effect will be to prevent the offender from obtaining employment on his release from any custodial sentence. This does not necessarily mean that the court should not impose a disqualification which will remain in force after the offender's release, if he has not previously been employed in a capacity in which driving is essential.

There is no minimum or maximum period of disqualification.

Disqualification Order

CRIMINAL JUSTICE AND COURT SERVICES ACT 2000 s.26

References: Current Sentencing Practice H7–1; Archbold 5–1119

Disqualification orders are abolished in all cases with effect from June 17, 2013.

Drink Banning Order

VIOLENT CRIME REDUCTION ACT 2006 s.6

References: Archbold 5–1093

A court may make a drink banning order against a person aged 16 or over who is convicted of an offence which was committed when he was under the influence of alcohol.

The court must consider whether the offender has engaged in **criminal or disorderly conduct while under the influence of alcohol** since the commencement of the Violent Crime Reduction Act 2006 s.3, and whether a drink banning order is necessary to protect other persons from further **criminal or disorderly conduct while he is under the influence of alcohol**.

If the court decides that the offender was under the influence of alcohol at the time of the offence, but that he has not engaged in criminal or disorderly conduct while under the influence of alcohol since the commencement of the Violent Crime Reduction Act 2006 s.3, or that a drink banning order is not necessary to protect other persons from further criminal or disorderly conduct while he is under the influence of alcohol, it **must state in open court that it has so decided** and give its reasons.

If the court decides that the offender was under the influence of alcohol at the time of the offence, and that he has engaged in criminal or disorderly conduct while under the influence of alcohol since the commencement of the Violent Crime Reduction Act 2006 s.3, and that a drink banning order is necessary to protect other persons from further criminal or disorderly conduct while he is under the influence of alcohol, but does not make a drink banning order, it **must give its reasons for not doing so in open court**.

A drink banning order prohibits the person against whom it is made from doing the things described in the order. It may impose *any prohibition which is necessary for the purpose of protecting other persons from criminal or disorderly conduct by the offender while he is under the influence of alcohol.*

The prohibitions must include such prohibitions as the court considers necessary on the offender's entering licenced premises or other premises where alcohol is available.

The order may not prohibit the offender from having access to a place where he resides, where he is required to attend for the purposes of work or employment, where he is expected to attend for the purposes of education or medical treatment, or where he is required to attend by any obligation imposed on him by any enactment or order of a court or tribunal.

A drink banning order lasts for **at least six months and not more than two years**. Different prohibitions may last for different periods, and the order may provide that the whole order, or any prohibition, may cease to have effect after a specified period, not less than half of the period specified in the original order, if the offender satisfactorily completes an approved course.

A drink banning order takes effect on the day on which it is made, or on the day on which the offender is released from custody.

A provision that the order or a prohibition in it may cease to have effect if the offender attends an approved course may be made only if a place on the specified approved course is available, and the offender has agreed to its inclusion in the order. The court must explain the effect of including the provision in the order, the requirements of the course and any fees which the offender will be liable to pay. If the court makes a drink banning order without a provision that the order or a prohibition in it may cease to have effect if the offender attends an approved course, it must **give its reasons for not including the provision in open court**.

A court considering whether to make a drink banning order may consider evidence led by the prosecution and by the defence, whether or not the evidence would have been admissible in the proceedings in which the offender was convicted.

A drink banning order may be made only in addition to a sentence or a conditional discharge.

Proceedings may be adjourned after sentence for the purpose of making a drink banning order. An interim drink banning order may be made.

A drink banning order may be varied, discharged or extended on application, so long as the order does not extend beyond two years.

Breach of a drink banning order is as **summary offence punishable with a fine at level 4**.

Repeal

The provisions relating to imposing a drinking banning order on conviction were repealed by the Anti-social Behaviour, Crime and Policing Act 2014, with effect from October 20, 2014. The repeal applies to proceedings commenced on or after that date. For proceedings commenced before that date, an order remains available.

Existing orders remain in force and may be varied or discharged, but the length of the order cannot be extended.

Breach proceedings are unaffected.

Early Release—Criminal Justice Act 2003

CRIMINAL JUSTICE ACT 2003 ss.237–268

References: Current Sentencing Practice A7A; Archbold 5–617

These provisions apply to all prisoners sentenced on or after December 3, 2012, irrespective of the date on which the offence for which they were sentenced was committed.

An offender serving a sentence of imprisonment, detention in a young offender institution or detention under the P.C.C.(S.)A. 2000 s.91 for a term or total term of **less than twelve months** must be released unconditionally after serving one half of the sentence. Offenders released from sentences of detention in a young offender institution or detention under the P.C.C.(S.)A. 2000 s.91 are subject to supervision following release for three months in accordance with the Criminal Justice Act 2003 s.256B.

An offender sentenced to imprisonment, detention in a young offender institution or detention under the P.C.C.(S.)A. 2000 s.91, for a term of 12 months or more will be released on licence after serving half of the sentence imposed by the court (the "requisite custodial period") and will remain on licence until the end of the whole term of the sentence.

Home detention curfew

A prisoner who has served at least one half of the "requisite custodial period" (which is one half of the nominal sentence) may be released on home detention curfew provided that the requisite custodial period is at least six weeks and the prisoner has served at least four weeks. The effect of this limitation is that the home detention curfew scheme applies only to offenders sentenced to a custodial sentence of at least 12 weeks. Provided such a prisoner has served one quarter of the nominal sentence or four weeks, he may be released up to 135 days before the date on which he would be otherwise be entitled to be released (the half way point in his sentence).

The home detention curfew scheme does not apply to offenders sentenced to four years' imprisonment or more, extended sentences of imprisonment or detention, or to certain categories of offenders listed in s.246(4).

An offender serving a sentence of 12 months or more who is released under this scheme must be subject to the standard licence conditions and to a curfew condition; he may also be subject to other conditions of a kind prescribed by the Secretary of State. The curfew condition remains in force until the day on which the offender would otherwise be entitled to be released from custody. It must require that the offender remains at a specified place for periods of not less than nine hours each day, and must provide for electronic monitoring of his whereabouts during the specified periods.

A person released on home detention curfew may have his licence revoked if he fails to comply with any condition of his licence, or if his whereabouts can no longer be monitored electronically. He must be informed of the reasons for the revocation and may make representations about the revocation to the Secretary of State, but he does not have the right to ask for his case to be reviewed by the Parole Board. If the Secretary of State does not reverse his decision to revoke the licence, the prisoner will remain in custody until the date on which he would otherwise have been released.

Licence conditions

Where a fixed term prisoner serving a sentence of 12 months or more is released on licence, the licence must include the standard conditions prescribed by the Secretary of State and such other conditions as may be specified. It may also include conditions relating to drug testing or electronic monitoring.

Recall

The Secretary of State may revoke the licence of a person who has been released on licence and recall him to custody. No particular conditions must be specified before this power is exercised.

On his return to custody, the prisoner must be informed of the reason for his recall and may make representations about his recall. His case must be referred to the Parole Board. If the Board does not recommend his immediate release, the Board must either fix a date for his release or fix a date for the next review of his case. The review must take place not later than one year after the decision to fix the date has been made. If the prisoner is not recommended for release at a later review, he will remain in custody until the end of the sentence.

Prisoners who are not serving extended sentences or sentences imposed for offences which are specified offences for the purposes of the Criminal Justice Act 2003 Sch.15, may qualify for automatic release after 28 days from the date of return to custody.

Additional days

Prison rules may provide for the award of "additional days" for disciplinary offences committed while in custody. Such days must be added to the length of time which must be served before the prisoner becomes entitled to or eligible for release, and are carried forward into the licence period.

Concurrent and consecutive sentences

Where an offender is sentenced to terms of imprisonment which are wholly or partly concurrent, the offender does not become eligible for or entitled to be released from any of the sentences before the date on which he would be eligible for or entitled to be released from each of the other sentences.

Where an offender is sentenced to consecutive terms, whether they are imposed on the same occasion or different occasions, he is not entitled to be released until he has served half of the aggregate term, and will remain on licence until the end of the aggregate term.

Recommending licence conditions

When a court passes a sentence of imprisonment or detention in a young offender institution for 12 months or more (but not a sentence of detention under the P.C.C.(S.)A. 2000 s.91) it may "recommend . . . any particular conditions which in its view should be included in any licence granted to the offender." The recommendation is not binding on the Secretary of State and does not form part of the sentence "for any purpose". It is therefore not subject to appeal. The recommendation will be considered by the Secretary of State when the offender is released at the half way point in the sentence, or if he is released on licence at any other stage—under the home detention curfew scheme, or on compassionate grounds.

Exclusion Orders (Licensed Premises)

LICENSED PREMISES (EXCLUSION OF CERTAIN PERSONS) ACT 1980

References: Current Sentencing Practice H4–1; Archbold 5–1090

If the offender has been convicted of an offence **committed on licensed premises** in the course of which he made **resort to violence**, the court may make an exclusion order. The order prohibits the offender from entering the **licensed premises specified** in the order without the express consent of the licensee or his servant or agent.

The order may be made in respect of any licensed premises, whether or not the offender has committed an offence in those premises, but **all the premises to which the order applies must be specified in the order**.

An exclusion order may be made in addition to any other form of sentence or order including a discharge. An exclusion order may not be made as the only sentence of order for the offence.

The court must fix the term of the order. The minimum term is three months; the maximum term is two years.

Note: the Licensed Premises (Exclusion of Certain Persons) Act 1980 is repealed by the Violent Crime Reduction Act 2006, Sch.5. That repeal was not in force on November 13, 2014.

Extradited Offenders

CRIMINAL JUSTICE ACT 2003 s.243(2)

If the offender has been sentenced after having been extradited to the United Kingdom and without having been first restored or had an opportunity of leaving the United Kingdom, and he was kept in custody while he was awaiting his extradition for any period, the court by which he is sentenced must specify in open court the number of days for which he was kept in custody while awaiting extradition. These days count as time served as part of the sentence.

The sentencing court has no power to disallow any days spent in custody prior to extradition.

Financial Circumstances Order

CRIMINAL JUSTICE ACT 2003 s.162

References: Current Sentencing Practice J1–1; Archbold 5–672

Where an individual has been convicted of an offence, the court may, before sentencing him, make a financial circumstances order with respect to him, requiring him to give to the court, within such period as may be specified in the order, such a statement of his financial circumstances as the court may require.

A financial circumstances order may also be made by a magistrates' court which has been notified that an individual desires to plead guilty without appearing before the court, or by a court considering whether to make an order against the parent or guardian of a child or young person who has been convicted of an offence.

Failure to comply with a financial circumstances order, or making a false statement in response to a financial circumstances order, is a summary offence.

A court may make a financial circumstances order irrespective of the kind of sentence that it has in mind.

Financial Reporting Order

SERIOUS ORGANISED CRIME AND POLICE ACT 2005 s.76

References: Current Sentencing Practice J16–1; Archbold 5–1211

A court may make a financial reporting order when sentencing or otherwise dealing with a person for the following offences:

Obtaining by deception (Theft Act 1968 s.15);

Obtaining a money transfer by deception (Theft Act 1968 s.15A);

Obtaining a pecuniary advantage by deception (Theft Act 1968 s.17);

Procuring a valuable security by deception (Theft Act 1968 s.20(2));

Obtaining services by deception (Theft Act 1978 s.1);

Evasion of liability by deception (Theft Act 1978 s.2);

Any offence specified in the Proceeds of Crime Act 2002 Sch.2;

Fraud (Fraud Act 2006 s.1);

Obtaining services dishonestly (Fraud Act 2006 s.11);

Conspiracy to defraud*;

False accounting (Theft Act 1968 s.17)*;

Bribery (common law)*;

Corruption (Public Bodies Corrupt Practices Act 1889 s.1)*;

Bribes obtained by or given to agents (Prevention of Corruption Act 1906 s.1)*;

Assisting another to retain the benefit of criminal conduct (Criminal Justice Act 1988 s.93A)*;

Acquisition, possession or use of proceeds of criminal conduct (Criminal Justice Act 1988 s.93B)*;

Concealing or transferring proceeds of criminal conduct (Criminal Justice Act 1988 s.93C)*;

Concealing or transferring proceeds of drug trafficking (Drug Trafficking Act 1994 s.49)*;

Assisting another person to retain the benefit of drug trafficking (Drug Trafficking Act 1994 s.50)*;

Acquisition, possession or use of proceeds of drug trafficking (Drug Trafficking Act 1994 s.51)*;

Fund-raising for purposes of terrorism (Terrorism Act 2000 s.15)*;

Use and possession of money etc. for purposes of terrorism (Terrorism Act 2000 s.16)*;

Funding arrangements for purposes of terrorism (Terrorism Act 2000 s.17)*;

Money laundering in connection with terrorism (Terrorism Act 2000 s.18)*;

Acquisition, use and possession of criminal property (Proceeds of Crime Act 2002 s.329)*;

Cheating in relation to the public revenue*;

Fraudulent evasion of duty (Customs and Excise Management Act 1979 s.170)*;

VAT offences (Value Added Tax Act 1994, 72) (c.23) (offences relating to VAT)*;

Fraudulent evasion of income tax (Finance Act 2000 s.144)*;

Tax credit fraud (Tax Credits Act 2002 s.35)*;

Attempting, conspiring in or inciting the commission of, or aiding, abetting, counselling or procuring or any of these offences.*

Note: the section as originally enacted contained references to obtaining by deception (Theft Act 1968 s.15), obtaining a money transfer by deception (Theft Act 1968 s.15A) and obtaining a pecuniary advantage by deception (Theft Act 1968 s.17). References to these offences were repealed and replaced by references to offences of fraud and obtaining services dishonestly by the Fraud Act 2006 Sch.1, with effect from January 15, 2007. No express provision is made dealing with the question whether an order may be made after that date in respect of one of the offences specified in the repealed paragraphs committed before that date. The list of offences was extended to as to apply to attempts, conspiracies, incitements, and aiding and abetting of the offences listed. These provisions do not apply to the offences of obtaining by deception, obtaining a money transfer by deception, and obtaining a pecuniary advantage by deception.

*Offences marked with an asterisk were added to the list by the Serious Organised Crime and Police Act 2006 (Amendment of Section 76(3)) Order, 2007. This order came into force on May 4, 2007. It is uncertain whether an order may be made in respect of the offences added to the list by this order if the offence was committed before that date.

The court must be satisfied that *the risk of the offender committing another such offence is sufficiently high as to justify the making of a financial reporting order.*

The order has effect for the period specified, which must not exceed five years if the order is made by a magistrates' court, 20 years if the offender is sentenced to life imprisonment, or otherwise 15 years.

The effect of a financial reporting order is that the offender must make a report to a person specified by the court of such particulars of his financial affairs as may be specified, within the specified number of days at the end of the period or periods specified.

A person who fails to comply with a financial reporting order is guilty of an offence.

Fines

CRIMINAL JUSTICE ACT 2003 s.163

References: Current Sentencing Practice J1–1; Archbold 5–671

Crown Court

The Crown Court may impose a fine in lieu of or in addition to any other form of sentence, except a discharge, for any offence other than murder.

A fine may not be imposed in place of a sentence required to be imposed by the P.C.C.(S.)A. 2000 ss.110 or 111, by the Criminal Justice Act 2003 ss.225 to 228, by the Prevention of Crime Act 1953 s.1A(5) or the Criminal Justice Act 1988 s.139AA(7).

There is no limit to the amount of the fine.

Before fixing the amount, the court must inquire into the offender's financial circumstances.

The court may make a financial circumstances order. (See **Financial Circumstances Order.**)

The amount of any fine must reflect the seriousness of the offence, and the court must take into account the circumstances of the case including, among other things, the financial circumstances of the offender, so far as they are known.

In the case of a corporation, the court is not obliged to inquire into the means of the offender but must take them into account as far as they are known.

Where the Crown Court imposes a fine it may allow time for payment and direct payment by instalments. Time for payment must be allowed unless the offender appears to have sufficient means to pay the fine immediately, or is unlikely to remain long enough at a fixed address to allow the fine to be enforced, or is simultaneously sentenced to, or is already serving, a custodial sentence.

The court must fix a term of imprisonment to be served in default of payment. (See **Default Terms—Crown Court.**) The default term is fixed in relation to the whole amount of the fine, not to individual instalments.

Magistrates' court

The magistrates' court may impose a fine not exceeding £5,000 for any one either-way offence unless special provision is made for a larger fine. There is no limit on the amount of the aggregate fine imposed for a number of different offences.

A magistrates' court may impose a fine for a summary offence subject to the maximum fine provided for the offence by reference to the standard scale. There is no limit to the aggregate amount which may be imposed for a number of separate offences.

The standard scale is:

Level 1 £200
Level 2 £500
Level 3 £1,000
Level 4 £2,500
Level 5 £5,000

The maximum fine which a magistrates' court may impose on an offender under 14 is £250, and on a person between 14 and 18 is £1,000.

A magistrates' court may allow time for payment and direct payment by instalments. Time for payment must be allowed unless the offender appears to have sufficient means to pay the fine immediately, or is unlikely to remain long enough at a fixed address to allow the fine to be enforced, or is simultaneously sentenced to, or is already serving, a custodial sentence.

A magistrates' court does not fix a term to be served in default on the occasion when a fine is imposed, unless the offender appears to have sufficient means to pay the fine immediately, or is unlikely to remain long enough at a fixed address to allow the fine to be enforced, or is simultaneously sentenced to, or is already serving, a custodial sentence.

The default terms for fines imposed by magistrates' courts are the same as for the Crown Court (see **Default Terms—Crown Court**) except that the maximum default term which may be fixed is 12 months.

Forfeiture Orders—Misuse of Drugs Act 1971

MISUSE OF DRUGS ACT 1971 S.27

References: Current Sentencing Practice J4–1; Archbold 27–118

The offender must be convicted of a drug trafficking offence (as defined in the Proceeds of Crime Act 2002 Sch.2) or an offence under the Misuse of Drugs Act 1971.

The court may order forfeiture of anything **shown to the satisfaction of the court to relate to the offence**. The offender may give evidence to show that the property is not related to the offence.

The court may not order forfeiture of intangible property or land or buildings.

If anyone claims to be the owner of the property or otherwise interested in it, he must be given the chance to show cause why the forfeiture order should not be made.

The court may order the property concerned to be destroyed, or dealt with in such manner as the court may order.

Property may not be forfeited on the grounds that it is the proceeds of offences of which the offender has not been convicted, or is intended to be used to facilitate the commission of future offences.

Where a court has postponed confiscation proceedings and proceeds to sentence the offender before making the confiscation order, it must not make a forfeiture order until the confiscation order has been made.

Forfeiture Orders—Terrorist Offences

TERRORISM ACT 2000 S.23, 23A, (AS SUBSTITUTED BY THE COUNTER-TERRORISM ACT 2008 S.34),120A (AS INSERTED BY THE COUNTER-TERRORISM ACT 2008 S.38), TERRORISM ACT 2006 S.7, 11A (AS INSERTED BY THE COUNTER-TERRORISM ACT 2008 S.38)

References: Current Sentencing Practice J8; Archbold 25–42

Where a person is convicted of an offence under **s.15(1) or (2) or 16** of the Terrorism Act 2000, the court may order the forfeiture of any money or other property which, at the time of the offence, the person had in their possession or under their control and which had been used for the purposes of terrorism, or they intended should be used, or had reasonable cause to suspect might be used, for those purposes.

Where a person is convicted of an offence under **s.15(3)** of the Terrorism Act 2000, the court may order the forfeiture of any money or other property which, at the time of the offence, the person had in their possession or under their control and which had been used for the purposes of terrorism, or which, at that time, they knew or had reasonable cause to suspect would or might be used for those purposes.

Where a person is convicted of an offence under **s.17 or 18** of the Terrorism Act 2000, the court may order the forfeiture of any money or other property which, at the time of the offence, the person had in their possession or under their control and which had been used for the purposes of terrorism, or was, at that time, intended by them to be used for those purposes.

Where a person is convicted of an offence under **s.17** of the Terrorism Act 2000, the court may order the forfeiture of the money or other property to which the arrangement in question related, and which had been used for the purposes of terrorism, or at the time of the offence, the person knew or had reasonable cause to suspect would or might be used for those purposes.

Where a person is convicted of an offence under **s.18** of the Terrorism Act 2000, the court may order the forfeiture of the money or other property to which the arrangement in question related.

Where a person is convicted of an offence under any of **ss.15—18**, the court may order the forfeiture of any money or other property which wholly or partly, and directly or indirectly, is received by any person as a payment or other reward in connection with the commission of the offence.

Where a person is convicted of an offence against:

Terrorism Act 2000 ss.54, 57, 58 or 58A, 59, 60 or 61;

Terrorism Act 2006 ss.2, 5, 6, 9, 10, or 11, or

an offence specified in Sch.2 to the Counter-Terrorism Act 2008 as to which the court dealing with the offence has determined that the offence has a **terrorist connection**;

or any **ancillary offence** related to these offences,

the court may order the forfeiture of any money or other property which was, at the time of the offence, in the possession or control of the person convicted and had been used for the purposes of terrorism, was intended by that person to be used for the purposes of terrorism, or the court believes that it will be used for the purposes of terrorism unless forfeited.

Before making a forfeiture order, the court must give an opportunity to be heard to any person, other than the convicted person, who claims to be the owner or otherwise interested in anything which can be forfeited. The court must have regard to the value of the property, and the likely financial and other effects on the convicted person of the making of the order (taken together with any other order that the court contemplates making).

Where a court makes a forfeiture order in a case where the offender has been convicted of an offence that has resulted in a person suffering personal injury, loss or damage, or any such offence is taken into consideration by the court in determining sentence, the court may also order that an amount not exceeding a sum specified by the court is to be paid to that person out of the proceeds of the forfeiture. The court may make, and only if it is satisfied that but for the inadequacy of the offender's means it would have made a compensation under which the offender would have been required to pay compensation of an amount not less than the specified amount.

Additional powers

Where a person is convicted of an offence contrary to the **Terrorism Act 2000 s.54**, the court may order the forfeiture of anything that the court considers to have been in the possession of the person for purposes connected with the offence.

Where a person is convicted of an offence contrary to the **Terrorism Act 2000 s.57**, the court may order the forfeiture of any article that is the subject matter of the offence.

Where a person is convicted of an offence contrary to the **Terrorism Act 2000 s.58**, the court may order the forfeiture of any document or record containing information of the kind mentioned in subs.(1)(a) of that section.

Where a person is convicted of an offence contrary to the **Terrorism Act 2000 s.58A**, the court may order the forfeiture of any document or record containing information of the kind mentioned in subs.(1)(a) of that section.

Where a person is convicted of an offence contrary to the **Terrorism Act 2006 s.6**, they may order the forfeiture of anything the court considers to have been in the person's possession for purposes connected with the offence.

Where a person is convicted of an offence contrary to the **Terrorism Act 2006 s.9 or s.10**, the court may order the forfeiture of any radioactive device or radioactive material, or any nuclear facility, made or used in committing the offence.

Where a person is convicted of an offence contrary to the **Terrorism Act 2006 s.11**, the court may order the forfeiture of any radioactive device or radioactive material, or any nuclear facility, which is the subject of a demand under subs.(1) of that section, or a threat falling within subs.(3) of that section.

Before making an order under these provisions, the court must give an opportunity to be heard to any person, other than the convicted person, who claims to be the owner or otherwise interested in anything which can be forfeited. The court may also make such other provision as appears to it to be necessary for giving effect to the forfeiture, including, in particular, provision relating to the retention, handling, disposal or destruction of what is forfeited.

Guardianship Order

MENTAL HEALTH ACT 1983 s.37

References: Current Sentencing Practice F2–1; Archbold 5–1236

The court may make a guardianship order provided that the offender is 16 or older and the court is satisfied on the written or oral evidence of two medical practitioners that the offender is suffering from mental disorder and the court is satisfied that the mental disorder from which he is suffering is of a nature or degree which warrants his reception into guardianship.

The court must be of the opinion, having regard to all the circumstances, including the nature of the offence and the character and antecedents of the offender that the most suitable method of disposing of the case is by means of a guardianship order.

A guardianship order may not be made unless the court is satisfied that the local authority or other person concerned is willing to receive the offender into guardianship.

The order must specify the form or forms of mental disorder from which the offender is suffering. At least two practitioners must agree that the offender is suffering from the same form of mental disorder.

The court may not impose a sentence of imprisonment, impose a fine or make a community order but may make such other forms of order as may be appropriate.

A guardianship order may be made despite the fact that the offender would otherwise qualify for a required minimum sentence under the Firearms Act 1968 s.51A, a prescribed custodial sentence under the P.C.C.(S.)A. 2000 ss.110 or 111, the Prevention of Crime Act 1953 s.1A(5), the Violent Crime Reduction Act 2006 s.29 or the Criminal Justice Act 1988 s.139AA(7), or a sentence of life imprisonment, or an extended sentence under the Criminal Justice Act 2003. **This exception does not apply to an automatic life sentence.**

Hospital and Limitation Direction

MENTAL HEALTH ACT 1983 ss.45A, 45B

References: Current Sentencing Practice F2–1; Archbold 5–1250

Availability: A direction under section 45A is not available for those under 21 at conviction: *R. v Fort* [2013] EWCA Crim 2332; [2014] 2 Cr.App.R.(S.) 24.

A court which passes a sentence of imprisonment for an offence other than murder on an offender may make a hospital and limitation direction, if the court is satisfied on the evidence of two medical practitioners (one of whom must give evidence orally) that:

(a) the offender is suffering from a mental disorder;

(b) the disorder is of a nature or degree which makes it appropriate for him to be detained in a hospital for medical treatment; or

(c) appropriate medical treatment is available for him.

The order must direct that the offender be removed to a hospital, and be subject to the restrictions set out in Mental Health Act 1983 s.41.

The hospital must be specified in the direction, and the court must be satisfied that the offender will be admitted to the hospital within 28 days of the making of the order.

An offender subject to a hospital and limitation direction will be treated as if he had been sentenced to imprisonment and transferred to hospital by order of the Secretary of State.

If the offender ceases to be in need of treatment before the expiration of the sentence, he will be liable to be returned to prison. If he is still in hospital when the period during which he is liable to be detained under the sentence expires, he will be liable to be detained in hospital as an unrestricted patient.

A hospital and limitation direction may be made in conjunction with a determinate sentence of imprisonment, a longer than commensurate sentence of imprisonment, a discretionary sentence of life imprisonment or an automatic sentence of life imprisonment. It may not be made in conjunction with a sentence of detention under P.C.C.(S.)A. 2000 s.91, or a sentence of detention in a young offender institution, or a mandatory life sentence imposed for murder.

Hospital Order

MENTAL HEALTH ACT 1983 s.37

References: Current Sentencing Practice F2–1; Archbold 5–1229

The court may make a hospital order provided that it is satisfied on the written or oral evidence of two medical practitioners that the offender is suffering from mental disorder and the court is satisfied that the mental disorder from which he is suffering is of a nature or degree which makes it appropriate for him to be *detained in a hospital for medical treatment.*

The court must be of the opinion, having regard to all the circumstances including the nature of the offence and the character and antecedents of the offender, and to the other means of dealing with him that the most suitable means of dealing with the case is by means of a hospital order.

A hospital order may not be made unless the court is satisfied that arrangements have been made for his admission to a hospital within 28 days of the making of the order.

The court may request any regional health authority to furnish such information as the authority has or can reasonably obtain with respect to hospitals in its region or elsewhere at which arrangements could be made for the admission of the offender.

The order must specify the hospital to which the offender is to be admitted and the form or forms of mental disorder from which the offender is suffering.

At least two practitioners must agree that the offender is suffering from the same form of disorder.

A hospital order may be made despite the fact that the offender would otherwise qualify for a required minimum sentence under the Firearms Act 1968 s.51A, a prescribed custodial sentence under the P.C.C.(S.)A. 2000 ss.110 or 111, the Prevention of Crime Act 1953 s.1A(5), the Violent Crime Reduction Act 2006 s.29 or the Criminal Justice Act 1988 s.139AA(7), or a sentence of life imprisonment or an extended sentence under the Criminal Justice Act 2003. **This exception does not apply to an automatic life sentence.**

Interim Hospital Order

MENTAL HEALTH ACT 1983 s.38

References: Current Sentencing Practice F2–1; Archbold 5–1235

The court may make an interim hospital order provided that it is satisfied on the written or oral evidence of two medical practitioners that the offender is suffering from mental disorder and there is reason to suppose that the mental disorder from which he is suffering is such that it may be appropriate for a hospital order to be made in his case.

An interim hospital order may be made only if a hospital place is available.

One of the practitioners on whose evidence the order is based must be employed at the hospital to be specified in the order.

An order may not be made unless the court is satisfied that arrangements have been made for the offender's admission to the hospital specified within 28 days of the making of the order.

An interim hospital order may be made for any period not exceeding 12 weeks in the first instance. The order may be renewed for further periods of 28 days at a time, if the court is satisfied that the continuation of the order is warranted. The order may not continue for more than 12 months in all.

An interim hospital order may be renewed in the absence of the offender provided that he is represented by a legal representative and his legal representative is given the opportunity to be heard. At the conclusion of the interim order the offender must be sentenced or dealt with by means of a hospital order or otherwise.

The court must give directions for the conveyance of the offender and his detention in a place of safety pending his admission to hospital.

The order must be terminated if the court makes a hospital order or decides after considering the evidence of the responsible medical officer to deal with the case in some other way.

A court may make a hospital order in the case of an offender subject to an interim hospital order in the absence of the offender, provided that he is represented by a legal representative and his legal representative is given the opportunity to be heard.

Legal Representation

P.C.C.(S).A. 2000 s.83

References: Current Sentencing Practice L6–1; Archbold 5–12

Statutory requirements relating to legal representation apply in the following cases:

(a) a sentence of imprisonment passed on a person who has not previously been sentenced to a sentence of imprisonment (for this purpose, a previous committal for contempt or in default, a suspended sentence, a sentence of detention in a young offender institution or detention under Children and Young Persons Act 1933 ss.53(2) and(3) or under P.C.C.(S.)A. 2000 s.91, does not count);

(b) a sentence of detention under P.C.C.(S.)A. 2000 s.91 passed on any offender, irrespective of previous sentences;

(c) a local authority residence requirement or a foster parent residence requirement in a supervision order. (See **Supervision Order**);

(d) a detention and training order;

(e) a sentence of detention in a young offender institution;

(f) a youth rehabilitation order containing either a local authority residence requirement or a fostering requirement.

A court must not pass such a sentence on a person who is not legally represented unless he has applied for legal representation and his application has been refused on the ground that his means are adequate, or he has refused or failed to apply for legal representation after being told of his right to do so.

A person is legally represented only if he has the assistance of counsel or a solicitor at some time after he has been found guilty and before he has been sentenced. It is not sufficient that the offender was represented at the trial, or when he pleaded guilty.

An offender who has dismissed his representatives after having advice between conviction and sentence may be sentenced while unrepresented, but the court must first withdraw any legal representation order.

A sentence passed in breach of these requirements is unlawful, but the Court of Appeal on an appeal against such a sentence may substitute a lawful sentence.

Life Sentence for Second Listed Offence

CRIMINAL JUSTICE ACT 2003 s.224A

If a person **aged 18 or over** is convicted of an offence listed in **Part 1 of Schedule 15B** to the Criminal Justice Act 2003, **committed on or after December 3, 2012,** and the **sentence condition** and the **previous offence condition** are met, the court **must** impose a sentence of life imprisonment (or custody for life if the offender is under 21) unless the court is of the opinion that there are *particular circumstances* which relate to the offence, the previous offence or to the offender which would make it **unjust** to impose a sentence of life imprisonment or custody for life in all the circumstances.

A life sentence must be imposed even though the offence concerned is not otherwise punishable with imprisonment for life.

The **sentence condition** is that the court would (in compliance with ss.152(2) and 152(3)—see **Custodial Sentences—Criminal Justice Act 2003—General Criteria**) impose a sentence of imprisonment or detention in a young offender institution for **10 years or more**, disregarding any extension period imposed under s.226A (see **Specified Offences—Adult Offenders**).

The **previous offence condition** is that **at the time the offence was committed** the offender had been convicted of an offence listed in Schedule 15B, and was sentenced to:

a **life sentence**, a sentence of custody for life, a sentence of imprisonment, detention in a young offender institution or detention for public protection with a **minimum term of at least five years,** disregarding any period by which the minimum term was reduced on account of time spent in custody on remand or on bail;

an **extended sentence** of imprisonment, detention in a young offender institution or detention with a custodial term of 10 years or more before the deduction of any time spent in custody on remand or on bail;

a **sentence of imprisonment**, detention in a young offender institution, detention under the Powers of Criminal Courts Act 2000 s.91, or any other form of detention, for **10 years or more** before the deduction of any time spent in custody on remand or on bail.

It is not necessary that the offender should have been 18 or over at the time when the previous offence was committed.

For the offences listed in Sch.15B, see p.260.

Magistrates' Courts' Powers—Custodial Sentence

MAGISTRATES' COURTS ACT 1980 ss.132 AND 133, P.C.C.(S.)A. 2000 s.78

References: Current Sentencing Practice A10–1; Archbold 5–460

Note: substantial amendments to the provisions summarised below are made by the Criminal Justice Act 2003. The amendments were not generally in force on November 13, 2014.

The following limitations apply to sentences of imprisonment. They do not apply to detention and training orders.

Summary offences

The maximum for any one offence is six months, or the maximum provided for the offence in question, if that is less. The maximum aggregate term for more than one summary offence is six months.

Either-way offences

The maximum term for any one offence is six months. The maximum aggregate term for more than one either-way offence is 12 months. The minimum term of imprisonment which a magistrates' court may impose is five days.

The restrictions on aggregate terms do not include activation of suspended sentences.

The restrictions do not apply to default terms fixed in respect of fines imposed on the same occasion as a custodial sentence is imposed, but they do apply where an offender is sentenced to a custodial sentence and committed in default on the same occasion.

The restrictions must be observed by the Crown Court when dealing with an offender in respect of the following matters:

(a) an offence for which he has been committed for sentence under P.C.C.(S.)A. 2000 s.6;

(b) an offence in respect of which the offender has been committed which a view to a restriction order under Mental Health Act 1983 s.43 and in respect of whom the Crown Court does not make a hospital order;

(c) an offence in respect of which a magistrates' court has made a community order which the Crown Court has revoked;

(d) an offence for which the Crown Court has power to deal with the offender under Criminal Justice Act 1988 ss.40 or 41;

(e) an offence in respect of which the offender has appealed against his conviction or sentence;

(f) an offence for which the offender is sentenced under P.C.C.(S.)A. 2000 s.4(5).

Maximum Sentence

References: Current Sentencing Practice A1–1; Archbold 5–480

The maximum sentence for an offence should normally be reserved for the most serious examples of that offence which are likely to be encountered in practice.

The maximum sentence should not normally be imposed for an attempt to commit an offence, or where the offender has pleaded guilty, or where there is substantial mitigation.

Consecutive maximum sentences may be properly imposed provided that each individual offence is one of the most serious examples of the type of offence, and the sentences are properly made consecutive. (See **Consecutive Sentences.**)

Where the maximum sentence for an offence is increased, the new maximum sentence will normally apply only to offences committed after the increase has taken effect. Where an offender has been convicted of an offence committed on a date unknown between two dates, and the maximum sentence has been increased between those two dates, the lower maximum sentence applies.

Where the offender has been convicted of an offence of a general nature, but the facts fall within the scope of a more narrowly defined offence for which a lower maximum sentence has been provided, the court should have regard to the lower maximum sentence, but is not necessarily bound by it.

Minimum Term

P.C.C.(S.)A. s.82A

References: Current Sentencing Practice A18–1K; Archbold 5–511

These provisions apply where the court passes any of the following sentences:

(a) a discretionary life sentence;

(b) a statutory life sentence under the Criminal Justice Act 2003 s.224A or s.225;

(c) a sentence of custody for life (otherwise than on conviction for murder);

(d) a sentence of detention under the P.C.C.(S.)A. 2000 s.91, for life;

(e) an automatic life sentence under the P.C.C.(S.)A. 2000 s.109.

They do not apply where the court passes a mandatory life sentence on a person convicted of murder.

In addition to passing the sentence, the court must normally specify the minimum period during which the offender will be required to remain in prison before becoming eligible for consideration by the Parole Board with a view to release.

The period is calculated by deciding what determinate term of imprisonment would have been appropriate if a sentence of life imprisonment had not been passed (the notional determinate sentence) and then specifying a period equal to between one-half and one-third of that term. Normally, the period should be equal to one-half of the term. *In certain exceptional cases the period may be more than one-half of the notional determinate sentence.*

In fixing the specified period, the court should give appropriate credit for a guilty plea.

If the offender has been convicted of more than one offence, the period should reflect the gravity of all of the offences of which he has been convicted, including those for which a sentence of life imprisonment is not passed.

If the offender has spent **time in custody on remand**, or awaiting extradition, the sentencer should deduct an appropriate amount of time from the specified period. The time deducted should not exceed the actual period spent in custody on remand. If the offender has been on bail subject to a qualifying curfew, the court should deduct half the number of days spent on bail subject to curfew, if the Criminal Justice Act s.240A would have applied to those days.

If the offender was **over 21 when the offence was committed** and is sentenced to life imprisonment, the court need not specify a period if it is of the opinion that no period should be specified because of seriousness of the offence or offences concerned.

If an offender who is serving the minimum term of an indeterminate sentence falls to be sentenced for another offence, the court may impose a determinate sentence to begin at the expiry of the minimum term of the indeterminate sentence.

Where a court is sentencing an offender to a life sentence and also sentencing him for other offences which are not specified offences, the court may calculate the notional determinate sentence for the specified offence by reference to the seriousness of all the offences.

Murder

CRIMINAL JUSTICE ACT 2003 s.269

References: Current Sentencing Practice B0–1; Archbold 5–399

A person convicted of murder who is aged 21 on the date of conviction must be sentenced to imprisonment for life, unless he was under 18 on the date when the offence was committed.

A person convicted of murder who is aged under 21 and over 18 on the date of conviction, must be sentenced to custody for life, unless he was under 18 on the date when the offence was committed.

A person convicted of murder who was under 18 on the date when the offence was committed must be sentenced to be detained during Her Majesty's Pleasure, *irrespective of his age on the date of conviction.*

In all cases, a court which imposes a mandatory life sentence on a person convicted of murder must order that the early release provisions shall apply to him after he has served a part of the sentence specified by the court, unless the offender is over 21 and the seriousness of the offence or offences concerned is such that a "whole life order" must be made.

In deciding what part of the life sentence to specify, the court must have regard to the general principles set out in the Criminal Justice Act 2003 Sch.21, and any guidelines relating to offences in general which are relevant to the case and are not incompatible with the provisions of Sch.21.

Having identified an appropriate starting point in accordance with Sch.21, the court must take into account any aggravating or mitigating factors, to the extent that it has not allowed for them in its choice of starting point, and specify a minimum term which it considers appropriate to the seriousness of the offence or offences concerned. The minimum term may be of any length (whatever the starting point).

The court should deduct from the minimum term a number of days equal to the number of days spent in custody on remand, unless the days would not have counted as remand days if the sentence had been a determinate sentence. If the offender has been on bail subject to a qualifying curfew, the court should deduct half the number of days spent on bail subject to curfew, if the Criminal Justice Act s.240A or the Criminal Justice and Immigration Act 2008 Sch.6 would have applied to those days.

In the case of a person sentenced to custody for life or imprisonment for life (but not detention during Her Majesty's Pleasure) for an offence committed before December 18, 2003, the minimum term must not be greater than the term which under the practice followed by the Secretary of State before December 2002, the Secretary of State would have been likely to have specified.

On passing sentence, the court must state in open court, in ordinary language, its reasons for deciding on the order made, and in particular must state which of the starting points in Sch.21 it has chosen and its reasons for doing so, and why it has departed from that starting point.

Newton Hearings

References: Current Sentencing Practice L2–2; Archbold 5–99

The purpose of a Newton hearing is to determine factual issues which are relevant to the sentence and which have not been resolved by the offender's plea of guilty to the charges in the indictment.

If the defendant intends to plead guilty to a charge on a basis of facts that differs significantly from that on which the prosecution will rely, the defendant's representatives must inform the prosecution and where the plea is entered, the judge must be informed of the basis of the plea.

Where the prosecution agree that a plea will be accepted on a particular basis of fact, it is desirable that the basis on which the plea is entered should be recorded in writing.

The judge is not bound to accept a plea offered by a defendant on a particular basis, even though the prosecution have agreed to accept the plea on that basis. The judge may direct that a hearing should take place. If this occurs the defendant is not entitled to withdraw his plea and counsel for the prosecution must present the evidence to the court.

Where the defendant offers a plea on a basis which is not acceptable to the prosecution, and the issue cannot be resolved by amending the indictment, the judge must either hear evidence and determine the issue of fact, or sentence on the basis put forward by the defendant.

Such a hearing is limited to the determination of matters which are consistent with the terms of the counts in the indictment to which the defendant has pleaded guilty. It is not open to the prosecution to allege that the defendant is guilty of more offences than are charged in the indictment or taken into consideration, or that the offence committed was more serious than the offence charged in the indictment.

The hearing is conducted in the form of a trial without a jury. Evidence is adduced and witnesses are examined in the normal way. The judge should not intervene in the examination of witnesses.

The judge should direct himself that the prosecution must establish their version of the facts to the criminal standard of proof.

It is not necessary for the judge to hear evidence if the matter in issue is not relevant to sentence, or the defendant's story can be considered wholly false or manifestly implausible, or where the matters put forward by the defendant relate to personal mitigation only.

If a defendant puts forward a plea on a particular basis of fact, but that basis is rejected by the judge after hearing evidence, the defendant may lose some of the discount that he would otherwise expect for his plea.

Offences Taken into Consideration

References: Current Sentencing Practice L3–1; Archbold 5–160; Offences Taken Into Consideration and Totality Definitive Guideline (2012)

Where an offender admits an offence with which he has not been charged and asks the court to take it into consideration, the court may take account of that offence when passing sentence for the offence of which the offender has been convicted, but there is no conviction for the offence taken into consideration and the powers of the court depend on the offences of which the offender has been convicted, except as indicated below.

A compensation order or confiscation order may be made in relation to an offence that is taken into consideration.

An offence should not normally be taken into consideration if the court would not have power to deal with the offender for the offence, or if the offence would result in a mandatory sentence.

The offender should be shown a list of all the offences which he wishes to have taken into consideration; if he does not wish to have all the offences taken into consideration, he should be asked to indicate personally and specifically which offences he does wish to have taken into consideration.

Where an offender is committed to the Crown Court for sentence, the Crown Court may take offences into consideration only if the defendant admits the offences and asks for them to be taken into consideration when he appears before the Crown Court.

Where an offender admits that the offences to which he has pleaded guilty are specimen offences representing a larger number of offences which are not separately identified, those other offences are not "offences taken into consideration".

Parenting Order

CRIME AND DISORDER ACT 1998 s.8

References: Current Sentencing Practice E8A–1; Archbold 5–1282

A parenting order may be made only if the court has been notified that arrangements for implementing the order are available in the relevant area.

A parenting order may be made against the parent or guardian of a child or young person convicted of an offence or in certain other cases.

"Guardian" includes any person who in the opinion of the court has for the time being the charge of or control over the child or young person.

The order must require the parent or guardian to comply, for a period not exceeding 12 months, with such requirements as the court may consider desirable in the interests of preventing the commission of a further offence. The order must also include a requirement to attend for a period, not exceeding three months, counselling or guidance sessions, unless the parent has previously been the subject of a parenting order.

Unless the court makes a referral order, a court must make a parenting order in respect of a child or young person under the age of 16 who is convicted of an offence, or state in open court that a parenting order would not be desirable in the interests of preventing the commission of any further offence by the child or young person, and why not. The court may make both a referral order and a parenting order after considering a report from an appropriate officer.

The court must explain the effect of the order, the consequences that may follow a failure to comply with the requirements of the order, and the power of the court to review the order.

The consent of the parent or guardian is not required.

Parents and Guardians

P.C.C.(S.)A. 2000 ss.136–138, 150

References: Current Sentencing Practice E8–1; Archbold 5–1276

Where a person **under 16** is found guilty of an offence, and the court considers that the matter should be dealt with by means of a fine, costs or compensation order, the court **must** order the fine, costs or compensation order to be paid by the offender's parent or guardian, unless the parent or guardian cannot be found or it would be **unreasonable to make an order for payment**.

Where a person **over 16 but under 18** is found guilty of an offence, and the court considers that the matter should be dealt with by means of a fine, costs or compensation order, the court **may** order the fine, costs or compensation order to be paid by the offender's parent or guardian, unless the parent or guardian cannot be found or it would be **unreasonable to make an order for payment**.

The parent or guardian must be given the opportunity to be heard before the order is made.

In considering the means of the offender for the purpose of such an order, the court should consider the means of the parent or guardian, rather than the means of the offender.

A court should not make an order against a parent or guardian on the basis that the offender has been neglected unless there is evidence of such neglect. The court should not base a finding adverse to a parent or guardian on information disclosed by the parent or guardian for the purposes of a pre-sentence report.

Where the offender is in the care of a local authority, or living in local authority accommodation, and the local authority has parental responsibility, the court may make an order against the local authority. An order should not be made against a local authority unless the local authority has failed to do everything that it reasonably could have done to protect the public from the offender, and there is a causative link between the failure and the offence.

Where the offender is living in local authority accommodation on a voluntary basis, it will normally be unreasonable to make an order against the parent or guardian.

Where an offender under the age of 18 is found guilty of an offence, the court may (and if the offender is under 16, **must**) bind over the parent or guardian to take proper care and control of the offender, if it is satisfied that this would be desirable in the interests of preventing further offences by the offender. **If the court fails to exercise this power, it must state in open court that it is not satisfied that this would be desirable in the interests of preventing further offences by the offender**.

The recognisance may be in an amount not exceeding £1,000 and for a period not exceeding three years, or until the offender's 18th birthday, whichever is the shorter.

Before fixing the amount of the recognisance, the court must take into account the means of the parent or guardian, so far as they appear or are known.

If the parent or guardian refuses to be bound over, the court may impose a fine of £1,000. (See also **Parenting Order.**)

Prescribed Custodial Sentence—Burglary

P.C.C.(S.)A. 2000 s.111

References: Current Sentencing Practice A15–1; Archbold 5–444

A court which sentences an offender for a domestic burglary must impose a sentence of at least three years' imprisonment or detention in a young offender institution if:

(a) the burglary was committed on or after December 1, 1999;

(b) at the time when the burglary was committed the offender was 18 or over;

(c) at the time when the burglary was committed the offender had been convicted of two other domestic burglaries;

(d) each of the earlier domestic burglaries was committed on or after December 1, 1999;

(e) the offender had been convicted of the first domestic burglary before he committed the second.

A domestic burglary is a burglary committed in respect of a building or part of a building which is a dwelling. **A burglary may not be treated as a domestic burglary for this purpose unless the fact that it was committed in respect of a dwelling is alleged in the indictment or information.**

A conviction which has been followed by a conditional or absolute discharge does not count for these purposes. A conviction by a magistrates' court does count. A finding of guilt by a youth court does count. A conviction in any part of the United Kingdom other than England and Wales or any EEC Member State for an offence committed on or after April 15, 2010, which would amount to domestic burglary if done in England and Wales counts for this purpose.

Burglaries committed before December 1, 1999 do not count for the purposes of prescribed custodial sentences.

The offender must have been 18 or over at the time of the third burglary, but it is not necessary that he should have been 18 at the time of either of the earlier burglaries.

The court is not obliged to impose a sentence of three years if there are *particular circumstances which relate to any of the offences and which would make it unjust to do so in all the circumstances.* Where the court does not impose the prescribed sentence, it must state in open court what the circumstances are.

If the offender has pleaded guilty, the court may pass a sentence which is not less than 80 per cent of three years (876 days, slightly less than two years and five months).

If the court finds that there are particular circumstances which would make it unjust to impose the prescribed custodial sentence, the discount for the plea of guilty is not limited to 20 percent of the sentence which would have been appropriate following a contested trial.

If the offender qualifies for a hospital order under Mental Health Act 1983, the court may make a hospital order.

A burglary committed in circumstances in which the obligation to pass a minimum sentence applies is triable only on indictment.

Prescribed Custodial Sentence—Drug Trafficking Offences

P.C.C.(S.)A. 2000 s.110

References: Current Sentencing Practice A15–1; Archbold 5–443

A court which sentences an offender for a Class A drug trafficking offence must pass a sentence of **at least seven years' imprisonment** or detention in a young offender institution, if:

(a) the offence was committed on or after October 1, 1997;

(b) the offender was 18 or over when he committed the offence;

(c) he has been convicted on at least two separate previous occasions of a Class A drug trafficking offence;

(d) the second offence was committed after the conviction for the first offence.

It is not necessary that the two earlier offences should have been committed after the commencement of this section.

The following offences are "drug trafficking offences":

(i) producing, supplying or possessing with intent to supply controlled drugs (Misuse of Drugs Act 1971 ss.4(2), 4(3) and 5(3)). (NB. simple possession is not included);

(ii) assisting in or inducing the commission outside the United Kingdom of an offence punishable under a corresponding law (Misuse of Drugs Act 1971 s.20);

(iii) improper importation, exportation, or fraudulently evading the rohibition or restriction on importation or exportation of controlled substances whose importation or exportation is prohibited by Misuse of Drugs Act 1971 (Customs and Excise Management Act 1979 ss.50(2), 68(2) or 170);

(iv) manufacturing or supplying a scheduled substance, knowing or suspecting that it is to be used in the production of a controlled drug (Criminal Justice (International Cooperation) Act 1990 s.12);

(v) having possession of a controlled drug on a ship, or being concerned in carrying or concealing a controlled drug on a ship, knowing it is intended to be unlawfully imported or has been exported (Criminal Justice (International Cooperation) Act 1990 s.19);

(vi) inciting, attempting or conspiring to commit any of these offences or aiding, abetting, counselling or procuring the commission of any of them.

A conviction which has been followed by a conditional or absolute discharge does not count for these purposes. A conviction which has been followed by a probation order made before October 1, 1992 does not count. A conviction by a magistrates' court does count. A finding of guilt by a youth court does count. A conviction in any part of the United Kingdom at any time, or in any EEC Member State for an offence committed on or after April 15, 2010, which would amount to a class A drug trafficking offence if done in the United Kingdom counts for this purpose.

The court need not pass a sentence of seven years if there are "particular circumstances" which would make it "unjust to do so". If the court does not impose a sentence of seven years, the circumstances which make the sentence unjust must be stated in open court.

If the defendant has pleaded guilty the court may pass a sentence which is not less than 80 per cent of the seven years (2,045 days, slightly less than five years and eight months).

If the court finds that there are particular circumstances which would make it unjust to impose the prescribed custodial sentence, the discount for the plea of guilty is not limited to 20 percent of the sentence which would have been appropriate following a contested trial.

If the offender qualifies for a hospital order under Mental Health Act 1983, the court may make a hospital order.

A drug trafficking offence committed in circumstances in which the obligation to pass a minimum sentence applies is triable only on indictment.

Pre-Sentence Reports

CRIMINAL JUSTICE ACT 2003 s.159

References: Current Sentencing Practice A2–1; D1–1B01; Archbold 5–22

A pre-sentence report is a report made by probation officer or other appropriate officer to assist the court in determining the most suitable method of dealing with the offender. *A pre-sentence report need not be in writing, unless it is required before a court passes a custodial sentence on an offender under the age of 18 or is required to be in writing by rules made by the Secretary of State.*

The pre-sentence report must be disclosed to the offender or his representative, and to the prosecutor, if the prosecutor is a Crown Prosecutor, or represents the CPS, the Customs and Excise, the DSS, the Inland Revenue or the Serious Fraud Office. If the prosecutor is not of such a description (such as a local authority or private prosecutor), a copy of the report need not be given to the prosecutor if the court considers that it would be inappropriate for him to be given one.

If the offender is under 18, the court must give a copy of the report to any *parent or guardian* of the offender who is present in court, even though a copy has been given to the offender or his counsel or solicitor. If the disclosure to the offender or any parent or guardian of the information contained in the report would be likely to create a risk of significant harm to the offender, a complete copy of the report need not be given to the offender or his parents or guardians, but a full copy of the report must be given to the offender's counsel or solicitor.

Previous Convictions

CRIMINAL JUSTICE ACT 2003 s.143

References: Current Sentencing Practice A0–1; Archbold 5–70

This section applies irrespective of the date on which the offence was committed.

If the offender has one or more previous convictions, the court must treat each previous conviction as an aggravating factor if (in the case of that conviction) the court considers that it can reasonably be treated as an aggravating factor, having regard to the nature of the offence to which the conviction relates and its relevance to the current offence, and the time that has elapsed since the conviction.

"Previous conviction" does not include convictions which are deemed not to be convictions by provisions dealing with discharges and probation orders. Under the P.C.C.(S.)A. 2000 s.14(1), a conviction which results in a discharge is deemed not to be a conviction, subject to the qualifications set out in subss.(2) and (3). A conviction before October 1, 1992 which led to a probation order is also deemed not to have been a conviction (see the P.C.C.(S.)A. 2000 s.13). "Previous conviction" includes convictions by a court in an EEC Member State for an offence which would be an offence under the law of any part of the United Kingdom, and a previous conviction for a service offence.

A court is not required to treat convictions by a court outside the United Kingdom or Member States as aggravating factors, but may take them into account and treat them as aggravating factors if it considers it appropriate to do so.

Prosecution Costs

PROSECUTION OF OFFENCES ACT 1985 s.18

References: Current Sentencing Practice J6–1; Archbold 6–27

Where a person has been convicted, or the Crown Court has dismissed an appeal, the court may order him to pay such costs to the prosecutor as it considers to be just and reasonable. *The amount to be paid must be specified in the order.*

An offender should not be ordered to pay costs unless the court is satisfied that he has the means to pay the costs ordered, or will have the means within a reasonable time. An offender who is sentenced to custody should not be ordered to pay costs unless he has the means to pay immediately, or good prospects of employment on release.

The fact that an offender has pleaded guilty is a material factor in considering whether to order him to pay the costs of the prosecution, but it does not necessarily mean that an order is inappropriate. An offender should not be ordered to pay costs simply because he has refused to consent to summary trial.

The fact that the amount of costs is greater than the amount of a fine imposed for the offence is not necessarily a ground for objecting to the order, but the court should consider the overall effect of any combination of financial penalties.

The court does not fix any term of imprisonment in default, but may allow time for payment or fix payment by instalments.

If the amount of the order exceeds £20,000, the Crown Court has the power to enlarge the powers of the magistrates' court responsible for enforcing the order if it considers that the maximum default term of 12 months is inadequate. The court should make an order that the maximum term of imprisonment in default should be a figure taken from the following table:

Amount not exceeding	Maximum term
£50,000	18 months
£100,000	24 months
£250,000	36 months
£1 million	60 months
Over £1 million	120 months

Purposes of Sentencing—Adults

CRIMINAL JUSTICE ACT 203 s.142

References: Current Sentencing Practice A0–1; Archbold 5–61

A court dealing with an offender aged 18 or over must have regard to the following purposes of sentencing:

(a) the punishment of offenders;

(b) the reduction of crime (including its reduction by deterrence);

(c) the reform and rehabilitation of offenders;

(d) the protection of the public; and

(e) the making of reparation by offenders to persons affected by their offences.

This provision does not apply to an offence for which the sentence is fixed by law, or for which a mandatory minimum sentence is required by the Firearms Act 1968 s.51A, the Powers of Criminal Courts (Sentencing) Act 2000 ss.110 or 111, the Violent Crime Reduction Act 2006 s.29, the Prevention of Crime Act 1953 s.1A(5), the Criminal Justice Act 1988 s.139AA(7) or the Criminal Justice Act 2003 ss.224A, 225 or 226.

The provision does not apply to the making of a hospital order or hospital and limitation direction under the Mental Health Act 1983.

Purposes of Sentencing—Young Offenders

CRIMINAL JUSTICE ACT 2003 s.142A

References: Archbold 5–66

Note: this section was not in force on October 31, 2014.

A court dealing with an offender aged under 18 must have regard to the prevention of offending (or re-offending) by persons aged under 18, the welfare of the offender, and the following purposes of sentencing:

(a) the punishment of offenders;

(b) the reform and rehabilitation of offenders;

(c) the protection of the public; and

(d) the making of reparation by offenders to persons affected by their offences.

This provision does not apply to an offence for which the sentence is fixed by law, or for which a minimum sentence is required by the Firearms Act 1968 s.51A or the Violent Crime Reduction Act 2006 s.29(6).

The section does not apply to the imposition of a sentence of detention for life under the Criminal Justice Act 2003 s.226(2), or the making of a hospital order or a hospital and limitation direction.

Racially or Religiously Aggravated Crimes

CRIMINAL JUSTICE ACT 2003 s.145

References: Current Sentencing Practice A16–1; Archbold 5–119

A crime is racially or religiously aggravated if at the time of committing the offence, or immediately before or after doing so, the offender demonstrates towards the victim of the offence hostility based on the victim's membership (or presumed membership) of a racial or religious group or the offence is motivated (wholly or partly) by hostility towards members of a racial or religious group based on their membership of that group.

A "racial group" means a group of persons defined by reference to race, colour, nationality (including citizenship) or ethnic or national origins.

A "religious group" is a group of persons defined by reference to religious belief or lack of religious belief.

If the offence was racially or religiously aggravated, the court must treat that fact as an aggravating factor and must state in open court that the offence was so aggravated.

If an offender is convicted of a racially or religiously aggravated offence under Crime and Disorder Act 1998 ss.29, 30, 31 or 32, the court may in its discretion treat the racial or religious aggravation as an aggravating factor, but it is not bound to do so by s.145. The court is not bound to make the statement required by s.145(2)(b).

If the offender is convicted of an offence which could have been charged as a racially or religiously aggravated offence under Crime and Disorder Act 1998 ss.29 to 32 (such as unlawful wounding or assault occasioning actual bodily harm), but he has not been charged with the racially or religiously aggravated offence, or he has been acquitted of the racially or religiously aggravated offence, the court must not treat the offence as racially or religiously aggravated for the purposes of s.145.

Reasons for Sentence

CRIMINAL JUSTICE ACT 2003 s.174

References: Current Sentencing Practice L9–1AO1; Archbold 5–165

The court must state in all cases, in open court, in ordinary language and in general terms, its reasons for deciding on the sentence passed.

If the court passes a **custodial sentence**, the court must:

(a) identify any definitive guidelines which are relevant to the offender's case and if the offence was committed on or after April 6, 2010, explain how the court discharged any duty imposed on it by s.125 of the Coroners and Justice Act 2009, and where the court did not follow any such guidelines because it was satisfied that it would be contrary to the interests of justice to do so, state why it was so satisfied;

(b) if the court has reduced the sentence as a result of taking into account the offender's guilty plea, state the fact that it has done so.

If the court passes a **custodial sentence on an offender under 18**, the court must in addition state that it is of the opinion that the offence or the combination of the offence and one or more offences associated with it was so serious that neither a fine nor a community sentence can be justified for the offence.

If the court passes a **community sentence**, the court must:

(a) identify any definitive guidelines which are relevant to the offender's case and if the offence was committed on or after April 6, 2010, explain how the court discharged any duty imposed on it by s.125 of the Coroners and Justice Act 2009, and where the court did not follow any such guidelines because it was satisfied that it would be contrary to the interests of justice to do so, state why it was so satisfied;

(b) if the court has reduced the sentence as a result of taking into account the offender's guilty plea, state the fact that it has done so.

If the court makes a **youth rehabilitation order with intensive supervision and surveillance or fostering**, state that the court is of the opinion that the offence, or the combination of the offence and one or more offences associated with it, was so serious that, but for the power to make a youth rehabilitation order with intensive supervision and surveillance or fostering, a custodial sentence would be appropriate, and if the offender was aged under 15 at the time of conviction, the court is of the opinion that the offender is a persistent offender; if the offender is under 12, the court must state that a custodial sentence would be appropriate if he had been aged 12.

If the court imposes a **fine, discharge or any other sentence**, it must:

(a) identify any definitive sentencing guidelines relevant to the offender's case and if the offence was committed on or after April 6, 2010, explain how the court discharged any duty imposed on it by s.125 of the Coroners and Justice Act 2009, and where the court did not follow any such guidelines because it was satisfied that it would be contrary to the interests of justice to do so, state why it was so satisfied;

(b) if the court has reduced the sentence as a result of taking into account the offender's guilty plea, state the fact that it has done so.

In all cases, if the offence is **racially or religiously aggravated**, the court must state that that has been treated as an aggravating factor; if the offence has been aggravated by reference to the victim's **sexual orientation, disability, or transgender identity**, state that that the offence has been committed in such circumstances.

Explaining the effect of the sentence

The duty to explain the effect of the sentence applies to all sentences, including sentences fixed by law and required minimum sentences.

In the case of a **custodial sentence**, the court must explain "the effect of the sentence". This appears to require an explanation of the relevant provisions governing release and licence, which will vary according to the nature of the sentence imposed (life imprisonment, extended sentence, fixed-term sentence).

If the sentencing judge gives an inaccurate explanation of the effect of sentence, the inaccuracy of the explanation does not provide a ground of appeal against sentence.

In the case of a **community order**, the court must explain the requirements of the order, the effects of non-compliance, and the power of the court on application to vary the order.

In the case of a **fine** *(but not a compensation order or confiscation order)*, the court must explain the effect of the order and the effect of failure to pay the fine.

In the case of other orders (such as football banning orders, sexual offence prevention orders, disqualification from driving, etc.), the court must explain the effect of the order, the effect of non-compliance with the order, and any power of the court to vary the order.

Reasons for not making particular orders

In certain cases a court is required to explain in open court why it has not made an order of a particular kind, where it has power to do so.

These include:

Failure to make a compensation order;

Failure to impose an obligatory disqualification from driving;

Failure to make a drink banning order;

Failure to make a football banning order;

Failure to impose an automatic life sentence;

Failure to activate in full a sentence subject to a suspended sentence order.

Recommendation for Deportation

IMMIGRATION ACT 1971 S.6 AND SCH.3

References: Current Sentencing Practice K1–1AO1; Archbold 5–1256

A court should not make a recommendation for deportation in the case of an offender who is liable to automatic deportation. *A court should not normally make a recommendation in respect of an offender unless at least one of his offences justifies a sentence of twelve months' imprisonment or detention.*

A court may recommend for deportation an offender aged 17 on the day of conviction if he is not a British citizen and has been convicted of an offence punishable with imprisonment. The court may not recommend the offender for deportation unless he has been given seven days' notice in writing setting out the definition of a British citizen and explaining the exemptions from liability to be recommended for deportation. The court may adjourn to enable the required notice to be served. Failure to comply with this requirement does not necessarily mean that any recommendation will be quashed on appeal.

The court must not make a recommendation without a full inquiry into the relevant circumstances. Counsel for the offender must be specifically invited to address the court on the question of a recommendation. The court must give reasons for making a recommendation for deportation, if it does so.

The offender must be 17 years old by the day of his conviction. The offender is deemed to have attained the age of 17 at the date of his conviction if on considering any evidence he appears to have done so to the court.

If any question arises as to whether any person is a British citizen, or is entitled to any exemption, the person claiming to be a British citizen or to be entitled to any exemption must prove that he is.

The principal classes of persons exempted from liability to deportation are Commonwealth citizens and citizens of the Republic of Ireland who:

(a) had that status in 1973; and

(b) were then ordinarily resident in the United Kingdom; and

(c) had been ordinarily resident in the United Kingdom during the five years prior to the conviction.

The following principles are found in the cases:

(a) The principal criterion for recommending deportation is the extent to which the offender will represent a potential detriment to the United Kingdom if he remains in the country.

(b) The court is primarily concerned with his expected future behaviour, as evidenced by his offence and previous record.

(c) The court is not concerned with the political situation or conditions in the offender's home country.

(d) The fact that the offender is living on social security benefit is not a relevant consideration.

(e) The fact that the offender is not lawfully in the United Kingdom is not a relevant consideration, except in cases where he has secured admission to the United Kingdom by fraudulent means.

(f) The Court should not take into account the Convention Rights of the offender; the effect that a recommendation might have on innocent persons not before the Court; the provisions of Art.28 of Dir.2004/38; or the Immigration (European Economic Area) Regulations 2006 (SI 2006/1003).

If the court makes a recommendation for deportation, the court should consider whether to give a direction relating to the offender's custody or release pending the decision of the Secretary of State whether to make a deportation order on the basis of the recommendation.

If the court gives no direction for the release of the offender, he will remain in custody until this matter has been decided, irrespective of the type of sentence imposed by the court for the offence. The court may direct that the offender be released pending the decision of the Secretary of State, or released subject to such conditions as to residence or reporting to the police as the court may direct.

Referral Orders

P.C.C.(S.)A. 2000 ss.16–32

References: Current Sentencing Practice E14–1; Archbold 5–1275

(This passage summarises the law as it applies to offences committed on or after December 3, 2012.)

Where a defendant under the age of 18 appears for sentence before a youth court or magistrates' court for an offence punishable with imprisonment the court **must** make a referral order if:

(a) none of the offences is one for which the sentence is fixed by law;

(b) the court is not proposing to impose a custodial sentence or make a hospital order, or to grant a conditional or absolute discharge;

(c) the defendant has pleaded guilty to all the offences for which he is to be sentenced;

(d) the defendant has never been convicted by a court in the United Kingdom of any other offence;

(e) the offender has never been convicted by or before a court in another Member State of any offence.

The court **may** make a referral order if the offender pleaded guilty to the offence, or to at least one of those offences for which he is being dealt with, whether or not he has previously been found guilty of an offence.

Where the court makes a referral order, the court must not make a community order, impose a fine, grant a conditional discharge or make a reparation order for that offence. The court may make a compensation order. The court may not bind the offender over to keep the peace, or order his parents or guardians to be bound over. The court may make a parenting order after considering a report from an appropriate officer.

A referral order must specify the youth offending team responsible for implementing the order, require the offender to attend meetings of the panel established by the team, and specify the period (not less than three months and not more than 12 months) during which the contract is to have effect.

The court must explain the effect of the order and the consequences of non-compliance or breach.

Remand to Hospital for Psychiatric Treatment

MENTAL HEALTH ACT 1983 s.36

References: Current Sentencing Practice L7–1; Archbold 5–1234

The Crown Court may remand an accused person who is in custody awaiting trial or sentence to a specified hospital for medical treatment at any time before he is sentenced or otherwise dealt with for the offence. The power may not be used in the case of a person awaiting trial for murder.

The accused may be remanded before or after arraignment. The court must be satisfied on the written or oral evidence of two medical practitioners that the accused is suffering from mental disorder of a nature or degree which makes it appropriate for him to be detained in a hospital for treatment.

The accused may be further remanded without appearing in court if he is represented by a legal representative and the court is satisfied that a further remand is warranted.

The accused person may not be remanded or further remanded for a period exceeding 28 days at a time or for a total period exceeding 12 weeks. The court may terminate the remand at any time if it appears to the court to be appropriate to do so.

The court must give directions for the conveyance and detention in a place of safety of the accused pending his admission to hospital.

Remitting a Juvenile

P.C.C.(S.)A. 2000 ss.8–10

References: Current Sentencing Practice L13–1; Archbold 5–42

Where a child or young person is found guilty before the Crown Court of an offence other than homicide, the Crown Court must remit the offender to the youth court, unless it is satisfied that it would be undesirable to do so. It will be undesirable to remit if the judge who presided over the trial will be better informed as to the facts and circumstances, or if there would be a risk of disparity if defendants were sentenced by different courts, or if there would be delay, duplication of proceedings or unnecessary expense.

Where a child or young person is found guilty before a magistrates' court which is not a youth court, the magistrates' court must remit the offender to a youth court unless it proposes to deal with the offender by means of a discharge, a fine, or an order binding over his parents or guardians to take proper care and exercise proper control. This applies also to an offender who was a young person when the proceedings began.

Reparation Order

P.C.C.(S.)A. 2000 s.73

References: Current Sentencing Practice E11–1; Archbold 5–717

A reparation order may be made only by a court which has been notified that arrangements for implementing such orders have been made.

A reparation order is an order requiring an offender to make reparation for the offence otherwise than by the payment of compensation.

The restrictions on liberty imposed by a reparation order should be commensurate with the seriousness of the offence, or the combination of the offence and associated offences.

A reparation order may be made against an offender under 18.

A court may not make a reparation order in respect of the offender if it proposes to pass a custodial sentence or to make a youth rehabilitation order or a referral order. A court may not make a reparation order in respect of the offender at a time when a youth rehabilitation order is in force in respect of him unless it revokes the youth rehabilitation order.

A reparation order may not require the offender to work for more than 24 hours in all, or to make reparation to any person without the consent of that person.

The requirements of the order must so far as possible, avoid conflict with the offender's religious beliefs or any community order to which he is subject, and with the times at which he normally works or attends school.

The reparation must be made within three months of the making of the order.

Before making a reparation order the court must obtain and consider a report indicating the type of work that is suitable for the offender and the attitude of the victim or victims to the requirements proposed to be included in the order.

The consent of the offender is not required.

Required Minimum Sentence—Possessing Prohibited Weapon

Firearms Act 1968 s.51A

References: Current Sentencing Practice A15A–1; Archbold 5–449

A court dealing with an offender for an offence under the Firearms Act 1968 s.5 **must** impose **the required minimum sentence** "unless the court is of the opinion that there are exceptional circumstances relating to the offence or to the offender which justify its not doing so".

The section applies to offences committed on or after January 22, 2004.

The section applies to all prohibited weapons except weapons designed to discharge noxious gas, liquids or other things, and various types of rockets as specified in s.5(1A)(b)–(g).

The duty to impose a required minimum sentence applies to offences under the Firearms Act 1968 ss.16 (possession of a firearm with intent), 16A (possession of a firearm with intent to cause fear), 17 (possession or use of a firearm to resist arrest or when arrested for a Scheduled offence), 18 (carrying a firearm with intent to commit an offence), 19 (carrying a firearm in a public place), and 20 (trespassing in a building with a firearm), where the firearm is a prohibited weapon to which s.51A applies, **if the offence was committed on or after April 6, 2007.**

The **required minimum sentence** is at least five years in the case of an offender aged 18 or over when offence was committed, or three years detention under the P.C.C.(S.)A. 2000 s.91, if the offender was over 16 but under the age of 18 when the offence was committed.

The court may not allow a discount for a plea of guilty if the effect of doing so would be to reduce the length of the sentence below the required minimum term.

If a person between the ages of 18 and 21 is convicted of one of the offences to which the requirement to impose a minimum sentence applies, **committed on or after May 28, 2007**, he must be sentenced to five years' detention in a young offender institution, unless there are "exceptional circumstances". If the offence was committed before that date, the obligation to impose the required minimum sentence does not apply. The obligation to impose the required minimum sentence of three years' detention does apply to an offender aged between 16 and 18 convicted of an offence committed before that date.

A person over 18 convicted of an offence under the **Violent Crime Reduction Act 2006 s.28**, must be sentenced to a minimum term of five years if the weapon concerned is one to which s.51A applies, subject to the same exceptions. A person over 16 and under 18 must be sentenced to a minimum term of three years.

Restitution Order

P.C.C.(S.)A. s.148

References: Current Sentencing Practice J3–1; Archbold 5–711

The court has power to make a restitution order if goods have been stolen and the offender has been convicted of any offence with reference to the theft. "Stolen" for this purpose includes obtained by deception or blackmail, or by fraud contrary to the Fraud Act 2006.

The court may order the offender to restore the stolen goods to any person entitled to recover them from him.

On the application of the person entitled to recover the goods, the court may order the offender to deliver or transfer to that person any other goods which directly or indirectly represent the stolen goods.

The court may order a sum not exceeding the value of the stolen goods to be paid to the owner of those goods from money taken out of the possession of the offender on his apprehension.

If any third party has possession of the stolen goods, the court may order him to restore them to the person entitled to recover them. If the third party has bought the goods in good faith from the person convicted, or lent money to him on the security of them, the court may order payment to that person of a sum not exceeding the purchase price of the goods, or the amount of the loan, out of money taken out of the possession of the offender on his apprehension.

The court may not make a restitution order unless all the relevant facts are admitted or appear from the evidence given at the trial and the witness statements or depositions. The court may not embark on its own investigations with a view to making a restitution order.

Failure to comply with a restitution order is a contempt of court; the court does not make any order dealing with failure to comply.

Restraining Order

PROTECTION FROM HARRASSMENT ACT 1997 ss.5, 5A

References: Current Sentencing Practice H12–1; Archbold 19–277f

Where a court is sentencing an offender for any offence of which he has been *convicted on or after September 30, 2009*, irrespective of the date on which the offence was committed, the court may make an order prohibiting the defendant from doing anything described in the order, for the purpose of protecting the victim of the offence, or any other person mentioned in the order, from conduct which amounts to harassment, or will cause fear of violence.

Both the prosecution and the defence may lead, as further evidence, any evidence that would be admissible in proceedings for an injunction under s.3 of the Act.

The order may be for a specified period or until further order.

The prosecutor, the defendant or any other person mentioned in the order may apply to the court which made the order for it to be varied or discharged by a further order. Any person mentioned in the order is entitled to be heard on the hearing of an application to vary or discharge the order.

Harassing a person includes alarming the person or causing the person distress.

"Conduct" includes speech.

A court before which a person is *acquitted* of an offence on or after September 30, 2009, may, if it considers it necessary to do so to protect a person from harassment by the defendant, make an order prohibiting the defendant from doing anything described in the order.

The order may be for a specified period or until further order.

The prosecutor, the defendant or any other person mentioned in the order may apply to the court which made the order for it to be varied or discharged by a further order. Any person mentioned in the order is entitled to be heard on the hearing of an application to vary or discharge the order.

Harassing a person includes alarming the person or causing the person distress.

"Conduct" includes speech.

Where the Court of Appeal quashes a conviction, it may remit the case to the Crown Court to consider whether to make a restraining order. Where the Crown Court allows an appeal against a conviction in the magistrates' court, the Crown Court may make a restraining order.

A court should not make a restraining order in respect of a person who has been acquitted of the offence or offences charged without giving the person notice of what order is sought and the evidential basis for the order, and allowing the person a proper opportunity to make informed representations as to the appropriateness of the proposed order.

Restriction Orders (Mental Health Act 1983)

MENTAL HEALTH ACT 1983 s.41

References: Current Sentencing Practice F2–1; Archbold 5–1242

A restriction order may be made only in conjunction with a hospital order. (See **Hospital Order**.)

The Crown Court may make a restriction order if it makes a hospital order in respect of the offender and it appears to the court, having regard to the nature of the offence, the antecedents of the offender and the risk of his committing further offences if set at large, that is necessary for the protection of the public from **serious harm** to do so.

A restriction order may be made only if at least one of the medical practitioners whose evidence has been taken into account has given evidence orally before the court.

In deciding whether to make a restriction order, the court is concerned with the seriousness of the harm which will result if the offender reoffends, rather than with the risk of reoffending.

The seriousness of the offence committed by the offender is not necessarily important for this purpose. An offender convicted of a relatively minor offence may properly be subjected to a restriction order if he is mentally disordered and dangerous. An offender convicted of a serious offence should not be subjected to a restriction order unless he is likely to commit further offences which will involve a risk of serious harm to the public.

It is not necessary that the offender should be dangerous to the public as a whole; it is sufficient if he is dangerous to a particular section of the public, or to a particular person.

The harm to which the public would be exposed if the offender were at large need not necessarily be personal injury.

It is the responsibility of the court, and not that of the medical witnesses, to determine whether a restriction order is appropriate.

Retrial

CRIMINAL APPEAL ACT 1968 SCH.2 PARA.2

References: Archbold 7–111

Where a person is convicted after a retrial *ordered by the Court of Appeal Criminal Division under the Criminal Appeal Act 1968 s.7*, the court may pass in respect of the offence any sentence authorised by law, not being a sentence of greater severity than that passed on the original conviction. The court may pass any sentence passed in respect of that offence on the original conviction notwithstanding that, on the date of the conviction on retrial, the offender has ceased to be of an age at which such a sentence could otherwise be passed.

If the offender is sentenced to imprisonment or other detention, the sentence begins to run from the time when a similar sentence passed at the original trial would have begun to run. In computing the term of the sentence or the period for which the offender may be detained, any time before his conviction on retrial which would have been disregarded in computing that term or period if the sentence had been passed at the original trial and the original conviction had not been quashed, and any time during which he was released on bail under s.8(2) of the Criminal Appeal Act 1968, is disregarded.

The judge should make appropriate orders in respect of any time spent on bail subject to a qualifying curfew condition, before the original sentence or the later sentence was imposed.

These provisions do not appear to apply to a venire de novo ordered by the Court of Appeal.

Sentencing Guidelines

Criminal Justice Act 2003 s.172

References: Current Sentencing Practice G2–1A01; Archbold 5–144

If the offence was committed before April 6, 2010, and the Sentencing Guidelines Council or Sentencing Council has issued a "**definitive guideline**", every court in sentencing an offender must "**have regard to**" any definitive guidelines which are relevant to the case.

The Act does not require courts to follow a "definitive guideline" without regard to the detailed circumstances of the individual case. The court has a **discretion** to depart from a guideline in any case where it considers it to be appropriate or just to do so, provided that the court can give **reasons for the departure**.

If the court decides that the appropriate sentence in a particular case is not one which is indicated by a relevant definitive guideline, the court must **state its reasons for deciding that the appropriate sentence is of a different kind or outside the range of sentences indicated by the guideline**. Where the court imposes a sentence which is consistent with a "definitive guideline", the general duty imposed by s.174(1)(a) to state the reasons for deciding on the sentence passed appears to include by implication a duty to refer to the guideline to which the court has had regard.

*A court **should not** have regard to draft guidelines issued by the Council as a preliminary stage in the process of consultation, or to any views expressed by the Sentencing Advisory Panel.*

Where a definitive guideline is published after an offence is committed, but before the offender is sentenced, there is no breach of art.7 of the European Convention on Human Rights if the sentencing judge takes the guideline into account.

If the offence was committed **on or after April 6, 2010**, the court **must**, in sentencing an offender or exercising any other function relating to the sentencing of offenders, follow any sentencing guidelines which are relevant to the offender's case, unless the court is satisfied that it would be **contrary to the interests of justice to do so.** For this purpose, guidelines include definitive guidelines published by the Sentencing Guidelines Council which were in effect on April 5, 2010, guidelines included in any judgment of the Court of Appeal given before **February 27, 2004**, which have not been superseded by definitive guidelines issued since, and guidelines issued by the Sentencing Council under s.121 of the Coroners and Justice Act 2009.

The duty to follow any sentencing guidelines which are relevant to the offender's case includes, in all cases, a duty to impose on the offender, in accordance with the offence-specific guidelines, a sentence which is **within the offence range**, and where the offence-specific guidelines describe categories of case, a duty to decide which of the categories most resembles the offender's case in order to identify the sentencing starting point in the offence range, but **does not include a separate duty to impose a sentence which is within the category range, where the guideline specifies a category range**.

The duty to identify the category range does not apply if the court is of the opinion that, for the purpose of identifying the sentence within the offence range which is the appropriate starting point, none of the categories sufficiently resembles the offender's case.

The duty to pass a sentence within the offence range is subject to the reduction in sentences for guilty pleas, ss. 73 and 74 of the Serious Organised Crime and Police Act 2005 (reduction or review of sentence in respect of assistance by defendants) and any other rule of law by virtue of which an offender may receive a discounted sentence in consequence of assistance given (or offered to be given) by the offender to the prosecutor or investigator of an offence, and any rule of law as to **the totality of sentences**.

The duty to follow the guidelines is subject to statutory provisions restricting the imposition of community sentences, restricting the imposition of discretionary custodial sentences, requiring that a custodial sentence must be for shortest term commensurate with seriousness of offence, and requiring that a fine must reflect seriousness of offence. The duty to follow the guidelines is also subject to the duty to have regard to the Criminal Justice Act 2003 Sch.21, in fixing the minimum term to be served by a person convicted of murder, and to statutory provisions fixing minimum sentences to be served for certain offences under the Firearms Act 1968 or the Violent Crime Reduction Act 2006, or for repeated drug trafficking and burglary offences.

The duty to follow the guideline does not restrict any power which enables a court to deal with a **mentally disordered offender** in the manner it considers to be most appropriate in all the circumstances.

The duty to impose a sentence within the offence range does not restrict the power of the court to impose an extended sentence. The duty to follow the guidelines does apply where the court is determining the notional determinate sentence for the purpose of determining the minimum term to be served in connection with the appropriate custodial term of an extended sentence.

In giving reasons for the sentence imposed, the court must **identify any definitive sentencing guidelines relevant to the offender's case** and explain how the court discharged any duty imposed on it by s.125 of the Coroners and Justice Act 2009, and where the court did not follow any such guidelines **because it was of the opinion that it would be contrary to the interests of justice to do so**, state why it was of that opinion.

Serious Crime Prevention Order

SERIOUS CRIME ACT 2007 ss.1–43

References: Current Sentencing Practice H13; Archbold 5–1148

These provisions came into force on April 6, 2008. They do not apply where an offender is sentenced after that date for an offence of which he has been convicted before that date, but it appears that they do apply where an offender is convicted after that date of an offence committed before that date.

The Crown Court may make a serious crime prevention order where person **aged 18 or over** is convicted of a **"serious offence"** or has been convicted of a "serious offence" by a magistrates court and committed to the Crown Court to be dealt with for the offence.

A serious crime order may also be made on application by the High Court in the case of a person who has been involved in serious crime.

An order may be made only in addition to the sentence is respect of the offence concerned, or in addition to a conditional discharge or absolute discharge.

An order may be made if the court has *reasonable grounds to believe that the order would protect the public by preventing, restricting or disrupting involvement by the person in serious crime in England and Wales.* The order may contain such prohibitions, restrictions or requirements as the court considers appropriate for protecting the public by preventing, restricting or disrupting involvement by the person concerned in serious crime.

A serious crime prevention order may be made **only on an application** by the Director of Public Prosecutions, the Director of Revenue and Customs prosecutions, or the Director of the Serious Fraud Office. *The Crown Court must give an opportunity to a person other than the offender to make representations,* if that person applies to do so, if it considers that the making of a serious crime prevention order would be likely to have a significant adverse effect on that person.

Proceedings in the Crown Court in relation to serious crime prevention orders are civil proceedings and *the standard of proof to be applied is the civil standard of proof.* The court is not restricted to considering evidence that would have been admissible in the criminal proceedings in which the person concerned was convicted and may adjourn any proceedings in relation to a serious crime prevention order even after sentencing the person concerned.

A serious crime prevention order is binding on a person only if he is present or represented at the proceedings at which the order is made, or a notice setting out the terms of the order has been served on him.

A serious crime prevention order may not require a person to answer questions or provide information orally or to answer any privileged question, or provide any privileged information or documents. An order may not require a person to produce any excluded material (Police and Criminal Evidence Act 1984 s.11). An order may not require a person to produce information or documents in respect of which he owes an obligation of confidence by virtue of carrying on a banking business unless the person to whom the obligation of confidence is owed consents to the disclosure or production or the order contains a requirement to disclose information or produce documents of this kind. An order may not require a person to answer any question, provide any information or produce any document if the disclosure concerned is prohibited under any other enactment.

A serious crime prevention order must specify when it is to come into force and when it is to cease to be in force. An order may not be in force for **more than five years** beginning with the date on which it comes into force. Different provisions of the order may come into force or cease to be in force on different dates.

A person who is subject to a serious crime prevention order, or an authority who has applied for an order, may appeal to the Court of Appeal in relation to a decision in relation to a serious crime prevention order. A person who has been given the opportunity to make representations in respect of an order may also appeal to the Court of Appeal.

If a person who is subject to a serious crime prevention order is convicted by the Crown Court of a serious offence, or is convicted by a magistrates' court of such an offence and committed to the Crown Court to be dealt with, the Crown Court may vary the order if the court has reasonable grounds to believe that the terms of the order as varied would protect the public by preventing , restricting or disrupting involvement by the person in serious crime in England and Wales. The Crown Court may vary a serious crime prevention order which has been made by the High Court.

If a person is convicted of an offence of failing without reasonable excuse to comply with a serious crime prevention order, the Crown Court may vary the order if it has reasonable grounds to believe that the terms of the order as varied would protect the public by preventing, restricting or disrupting involvement by the person in serious crime in England and Wales.

A serious crime prevention order may be made against an individual, a body corporate, a partnership or an unincorporated association.

Offences against the following provisions are **serious offences** for the purposes of serious crime prevention orders:

The court may treat any other offence as if it were a specified offence if it considers the offence to be sufficiently serious to be treated as if it were a specified offence.

Asylum and Immigration (Treatment of Claimants, etc) Act 2004 s.4;

Bribery Act 2010 ss.1, 2, 6;

Common law offences;

Assault with intent to rob (where the assault involves a firearm, imitation firearm or an offensive weapon); conspiracy to defraud; cheating the public revenue; bribery;

Control of Trade in Endangered Species (Enforcement) Regulations 1997, reg.8;

Copyright, Designs and Patents Act 1988 ss.107(1)(a), (b), (d)(iv) or (e), 198(1)(a), (b) or (d)(iii), 297A;

Criminal Justice (International co-operation) Act 1990 ss.12, 19;

Customs and Excise Management Act 1979 ss.15(2), 15(3), 68(2) (if the offence is committed in connection with the prohibition or restriction on the importation of controlled drugs, or if committed in connection with firearms or ammunition), 170;

Environmental Protection Act 1990 s.33;

Finance Act 2000 s.144;

Firearms Act 1968 s.3(1);

Forgery and Counterfeiting Act 1981 ss.14, 15, 16, 17;

Fraud Act 2006 ss.1, 6, 7, 9, 11;

Gangmasters (Licensing) Act 2004 s.12(1), 12(2);

Immigration Act 1971 ss.25, 25A or 25B;

Misuse of Drugs Act 1971 ss.4(2), 4(3), 5(3), 8, 20;

Prevention of Corruption Act 1906 s.1(1) (first or second offence only);

Proceeds of Crime Act 2002 ss.327, 328 and 329;

Public Bodies Corrupt Practices Act 1889 s.1;

Salmon and Freshwater Fisheries Act 1975 s.1;

Sexual Offences Act 1956 s.33A;

Sexual Offences Act 2003 ss.14, 48, 49, 50, 52, 53, 57, 58, 59, 59A;

Tax Credits Act 2002 s.35;

Taxes Management Act 1970 s.106A;

Theft Act 1968 s.8(1) (where the offence involves the use or threat to use a firearm, an imitation firearm or an offensive weapon), 17, 21;

Trademarks Act 1994 ss.92(1), 92(2), 92(3).

Value Added Tax Act 1994 s.72;

Wildlife and Countryside Act 1981 s.14;

Any offence of **attempting or conspiring** to commit any scheduled offence (other than conspiracy to defraud), or any offence under the Serious Crime Prevention Act 2007 with reference to a scheduled offence;

An offence of aiding, abetting, counselling or procuring the commission of an offence specified in the Schedule.

In relation to conduct before the passing of the Serious Crime Act 2007, the scheduled offences include any corresponding offences under the law in force at the time of the conduct.

Sexual Harm Prevention Orders

SEXUAL OFFENCES ACT 2003 ss.103A–103K (INSERTED BY ANTI-SOCIAL BEHAVIOUR, CRIME AND POLICING ACT 2014 s.113)

Note: On November 13, 2014, the following provisions had not been brought into force.

When these provisions are brought into force, SOPOs, Foreign Travel Orders and Risk of Sexual Harm Orders will be repealed. See **Sexual Offences Prevention Orders** for details.

General

Availability: A court may make an order where it deals with the defendant in respect of:

(a) an offence listed in SOA 2003 Sch.3 or 5,

(b) a finding that the defendant is not guilty of an offence listed in Sch.3 or 5 by reason of insanity, or

(c) a finding that the defendant is under a disability and has done the act charged against the him in respect of an offence listed in Sch.3 or 5. (SOA 2003 s.103A(1) and (2).)

Test: The court must be satisfied that the order is necessary for the purpose of:

(i) protecting the public or any particular members of the public from sexual harm from the defendant, or

(ii) protecting children or vulnerable adults generally, or any particular children or vulnerable adults, from sexual harm from the defendant outside the UK. (SOA 2003 s.103A(2)(b).)

Defendant subject to earlier order: Where a court makes a sexual harm prevention order in relation to a person who is already subject to such an order, the earlier order ceases to have effect: SOA 2003 s.103C(6).

Contents of the order

Prohibitions: A sexual harm prevention order prohibits the defendant from doing anything described in the order: SOA 2003 s.103C(1).

Length of prohibitions: The order may specify that some of its prohibitions have effect until further order and some for a fixed period. Different periods for different prohibitions may be specified: SOA 2003 s.103C(3).

Test for prohibitions: Prohibitions must be necessary for the purpose of:

(a) protecting the public or any particular members of the public from sexual harm from the defendant, or

(b) protecting children or vulnerable adults generally, or any particular children or vulnerable adults, from sexual harm from the defendant outside the UK. (SOA 2003 s.103C(4).)

Length of the order: A prohibition may have effect:

(a) for a fixed period of at least five years, or

(b) until further order. (SOA 2003 s.103C(2).)

Foreign travel prohibition: A prohibition on foreign travel contained in an order must be for a fixed period of not more than five years: SOA 2003 s.103D(1). A prohibition on foreign travel is one that prohibits travel to any country outside the UK, to any country outside the UK as specified or other than specified. Where an order prohibits travel to any country outside the UK, the order must also require the defendant to surrender all his passports: SOA 2003 s.103D(1)–(4).

Variations, renewals and discharges

Who may apply: (a) the defendant, (b) the chief officer of police for the area in which the defendant resides, or (c) a chief officer of police who believes that the defendant is in, or is intending to come to that officer's police area, may apply to a court to vary, discharge or renew an order: SOA 2003 s.103E(1) and (2).

Renewing or varying an order: An order may be renewed or varied so as to impose additional prohibitions on the defendant only if it is necessary to do so for the purpose of:

(a) protecting the public or any particular members of the public from sexual harm from the defendant, or

(b) protecting children or vulnerable adults generally, or any particular children or vulnerable adults, from sexual harm from the defendant outside the UK.

Any renewed or varied order may contain only such prohibitions as are necessary for this purpose: SOA 2003 s.103E(5).

Discharging an order: The court must not discharge an order before the end of five years beginning with the day on which the order was made, without the consent of the defendant and:

(a) where the application is made by a chief officer of police, that chief officer, or

(b) in any other case, the chief officer of police for the area in which the defendant resides. (SOA 2003 s.103E(7).)

Interim orders

An interim order is not available in post-conviction cases: SOA 2003 s.103F.

Notification requirements

Subject to notification requirements: Where a sexual harm prevention order is made in respect of a defendant who was subject to notification requirements under SOA 2003 immediately before the making of the order, and the defendant would cease to be subject to those notification requirements while the order has effect, the defendant remains subject to the notification requirements: SOA 2003 ss.80(2) and 103G(1).

Not subject to notification requirements: Where a sexual harm prevention order is made in respect of a defendant who was not subject to notification requirements under SOA 2003 immediately before the making of the order, the order causes the defendant to become subject to the notification requirements under SOA 2003 from the making of the order until the order (as renewed from time to time) ceases to have effect: SOA 2003 ss.80(2) and 103G(2).

Appeals

Against the making of an order: A defendant may appeal against the making of an order "as if the order were a sentence": SOA 2003 s.103H(1).

Against the variation etc. of an order: A defendant may appeal against the variation, renewal or discharge, or the refusal to make such an order:

(a) where the application for such an order was made to the Crown Court, to the Court of Appeal; and

(b) in any other case, to the Crown Court. (SOA 2003 s.103H(3).)

Breach

Offence: A person who, without reasonable excuse, does anything prohibited by a sexual harm prevention order, commits an offence. This includes a requirement to surrender all passports where a foreign travel prohibition prohibiting travel to any country outside the UK is included in an order: SOA 2003 s.103I(1) and (2).

Maximum sentence: five years' imprisonment: SOA 2003 s.103I(3).

Can't impose conditional discharge: Where someone is sentenced for breaching their SHPO, the court may not impose a conditional discharge: SOA 2003 s.103I(4).

Repeal of Sexual Offences Prevention Orders etc.

When the Anti-social Behaviour, Crime and Policing Act 2014 Sch.5, para.3(1) is brought into force, SOA 2003 ss.104 to 122 (sexual offences prevention orders and foreign travel orders) will be repealed.

Sexual Offences Prevention Order

SEXUAL OFFENCES ACT 2003 s.104

References: Current Sentencing Practice H11–1A; Archbold 20–323

A court dealing with an offender for one of the offences listed in Sch.3 or Sch.5 of the Sexual Offences Act 2003 may make a sexual offences prevention order if it is satisfied that *it is necessary to make such an order, for the purpose of protecting the public or any particular members of the public from serious sexual harm from the defendant.*

Where an offence is included in Sch.3 of the Act subject to conditions relating to the age of the offender or the victim, or the sentence imposed on the offender, those conditions may be disregarded in making a sexual offences prevention order.

The power may be exercised in relation to an offence committed before the commencement of the Act. "Protecting the public or any particular members of the public from serious sexual harm from the defendant" means protecting the public in the United Kingdom or any particular members of that public from *serious physical or psychological harm, caused by the defendant committing one or more offences listed in Sch.3.*

A court may make a sexual offences prevention order in respect of a person convicted of an offence which is a specified offence for the purposes of the Criminal Justice Act 2003 (see Specified Offences—Adult Offenders) notwithstanding that it has decided that the offender does not present a significant risk or serious harm from future specified offences and that accordingly a sentence of life imprisonment or an extended sentence is not required.

A sexual offences prevention order may prohibit the defendant from doing anything described in the order. The only prohibitions that may be included in the order are those necessary for the purpose of protecting the public or any particular members of the public from serious sexual harm from the defendant.

The order may have effect for a fixed period **(not less than five years)** specified in the order or until further order.

Sexual Offenders—Notification Requirements

SEXUAL OFFENCES ACT 2003 s.80

References: Archbold 20–263

A person is subject to the notification requirements of the Sexual Offences Act 2003 if:

(a) he is convicted of an offence listed in Sch.3;

(b) he is found not guilty of such an offence by reason of insanity;

(c) he is found to be under a disability and to have done the act charged against him in respect of such an offence; or

(d) he is cautioned in respect of such an offence.

The periods during which the offender is liable to the notification requirements are as follows:

A person who, in respect of the offence, is or has been sentenced to imprisonment for life or for a term of 30 months or more	**An indefinite period beginning with the relevant date**
A person who, in respect of the offence or finding, is or has been admitted to a hospital subject to a restriction order	**An indefinite period beginning with that date**
A person who, in respect of the offence, is or has been sentenced to imprisonment for a term of more than 6 months but less than 30 months	**10 years beginning with that date**
A person who, in respect of the offence, is or has been sentenced to imprisonment for a term of 6 months or less	**7 years beginning with that date**
A person who, in respect of the offence or finding, is or has been admitted to a hospital without being subject to a restriction order	**7 years beginning with that date**
A person who has been cautioned	**2 years beginning with that date**
A person in whose case an order for conditional discharge is made in respect of the offence	**The period of conditional discharge**
A person of any other description	**5 years beginning with the relevant date**

Where a person is under 18 on the relevant date, the periods are one half of those specified as fixed length periods. If an offender under 18 is sentenced to a detention and training order, the relevant period for the purpose of determining his liability to the notification requirements is the custodial part of the order (normally half of the term of the order). A person sentenced to a detention and training order with a term of more than 12 months is liable to the requirements for a period of five years; if the order is for any period not exceeding 12 months, the period of liability is three-and-a-half years.

Where the offender is sentenced to terms which are wholly or partly consecutive, the table applies to the effective length of the aggregate terms.

Where an offender under 18 is convicted of an offence within the scope of Sch.3 and sentenced in a manner which results in an obligation to notify, the court may direct that obligation shall be treated as an obligation of the parent.

The only function of the court is to state that the offender has been convicted of a sexual offence to which the Sexual Offences Act 2003 applies, and to certify those facts.

This is not a mandatory obligation, and failure to make a statement does not affect the offender's liability under the Act. The court is not obliged to inform the offender of his liability, or of the period during which it will continue.

The obligation to notify imposed by the Sexual Offences Act 2003 is not a relevant consideration in determining the sentence for the offence.

Sexual Orientation, Disability or Transgender Identity

CRIMINAL JUSTICE ACT 2003 s.146

References: Current Sentencing Practice A16A; Archbold 5—119

Note: this section does not apply to offences committed before April 4, 2005, or in respect of transgender identity to offences committed before December 3, 2012.

If at the time of committing the offence, or immediately before or after doing so, the offender demonstrated towards the victim of the offence hostility based on either the **sexual orientation** (or presumed sexual orientation) of the victim, or a **disability** (or presumed disability) of the victim, or the victim being (or presumed to be) **transgender**, the court must treat that as an aggravating factor.

The same applies where the offence was motivated (wholly or partly) by hostility towards persons who are of a particular sexual orientation, or by hostility towards persons who have a disability or a particular disability, or who are transgender.

References to being transgender include references to being transsexual, or undergoing or proposing to undergo or having undergone a process or part of a process of gender reassignment.

In any such case, the court must state in open court that the offence was aggravated in this way.

Specified Offences—Adult Offenders

CRIMINAL JUSTICE ACT 2003 ss.225–229

References: Current Sentencing Practice A18; Archbold 5–495

Life imprisonment

If an offender aged 18 or over on the date of conviction is convicted of a "specified offence" committed on or after April 4, 2005, and the court considers that there is a significant risk to members of the public of serious harm occasioned by the commission by him of further specified offences, the court **must** impose a sentence of life imprisonment (custody for life if the offender is under 21) if the offence is punishable with life imprisonment and the court considers that the seriousness of the offence, or of the offence and one or more offences associated with it, is such as "to justify the imposition of a sentence of imprisonment for life".

For specified offences, see p.310.

Serious harm means *"death or serious personal injury, whether physical or psychological"*.

The sentence of imprisonment for public protection has been abolished except for offenders convicted before December 3, 2012.

A court which imposes a sentence of imprisonment (or custody) for life must fix a minimum term in accordance with the P.C.C.(S.)A. 2000 s.82A. The offender may not be released until he has served the minimum term. See **Minimum Term**.

If an offender who was 21 when the offence was committed is sentenced to life imprisonment, the court may decline to fix a minimum term if it is of the opinion that, because of the seriousness of the offence or of the combination of the offence and one or more offences associated with it, no order fixing a minimum term should be made.

An offender sentenced to life imprisonment (or custody for life) will remain on licence for the rest of his life.

Extended Sentences

The court may impose an extended sentence of imprisonment or detention in a young offender institution on a person convicted of any specified offence if the court considers that there is a significant risk to members of the public of serious harm occasioned by the commission by him of further specified offences.

An extended sentence may be imposed whenever the offence was committed, and whether before or after April 4, 2005. If the offender was convicted before December 3, 2012, an extended sentence may be imposed under the provisions which were in force on the date the offence was committed.

An extended sentence of imprisonment (or detention in a young offender institution) may be imposed only if the offender had been convicted of an offence listed in the Criminal Justice Act 2003 Sch.15B before committing the latest offence, or the appropriate custodial term would be **at least four years.**

An extended sentence consists of two components: the "appropriate custodial term" and the "extension period". *The combined length of the two components must not exceed the maximum sentence for the offence.*

The appropriate custodial term is the determinate custodial sentence which would have been imposed if the case had not required an extended sentence. In determining this term, the court must comply with the general provisions governing the use of imprisonment, in particular s.153(2), which requires that the custodial term must be the "shortest term" that in the opinion of the court is commensurate with the seriousness of the offence or the combination of the offence and one or more offences associated with it. *The custodial term may not be increased beyond what is the shortest term which would be commensurate with the offence, on account of the offender's dangerousness.*

If the offender is to be sentenced for more than one specified offence, the appropriate custodial term may not be made up of consecutive terms, each of less than four years but amounting to four years in aggregate, but the sentencer may impose a single term of four years for any one of the offences (subject to the maximum term for that offence) to reflect the seriousness of all of the associated offences for which the offender is being sentenced on that occasion, even though a term of four years would not be commensurate with the seriousness of the particular offence for which it is imposed.

The extension period is a period of licence, which is "of such length as the court considers necessary for the purpose of protecting members of the public from serious harm occasioned by the commission by him of further specified offences". It must not be more than *five years* in the case of a specified violent offence or *eight years* in the case of a specified sexual offence.

When the Offender Rehabilitation Act 2014 s.8 is in force, there will be a requirement that the extended licence period be for a minimum period of one year.

An offender serving an extended sentence will be released on licence automatically after he has served *two thirds of the appropriate custodial term*, unless the appropriate custodial term is 10 years or more or the offence or one of the offences for which the sentence is imposed is listed in Schedule 15B, Parts 1 to 3. In these cases the offender will not be released unless the Parole Board has directed his release on the ground that it is no longer necessary for the protection of the public that he should be confined, or he has served the whole of the appropriate custodial term and has not been released on licence and recalled.

Assessing dangerousness (s.229)

In assessing whether there is a significant risk of serious harm from future specified offences, the court must take into account all such information as is available to it about the nature and circumstances of the offence, and may take into account all such information as is available about the nature and circumstances of any other offences of which the offender has been convicted by a court anywhere in the world. The court may take into account any information which is before it about any pattern of behaviour of which any of the offences of which the offender has been convicted forms part, and may take into account any information about the offender which is before it.

If an offender qualifies for a hospital order under the Mental Health Act 1983 s.37, the court may make such an order even though the offender otherwise qualifies for a sentence of life imprisonment, custody for life or an extended sentence of imprisonment or detention in a young offender institution.

The following offences are listed in the Criminal Justice Act 2003, Sch.15B:

1. Manslaughter.

2. An offence under section 4 of the Offences against the Person Act 1861 (soliciting murder).

3. An offence under section 18 of that Act (wounding with intent to cause grievous bodily harm).

4. An offence under section 16 of the Firearms Act 1968 (possession of a firearm with intent to endanger life).

5. An offence under section 17(1) of that Act (use of a firearm to resist arrest).

6. An offence under section 18 of that Act (carrying a firearm with criminal intent).

7. An offence of robbery under section 8 of the Theft Act 1968 where, at some time during the commission of the offence, the offender had in his possession a firearm or an imitation firearm within the meaning of the Firearms Act 1968.

   Where the question arises whether a robbery committed was an "offence of robbery under section 8 of the Theft Act 1968 where, at some time during the commission of the offence, the offender had in his possession a firearm or an imitation firearm within the meaning of the Firearms Act 1968", it must be established or admitted that the offender was a party to the robbery which to his knowledge involved the possession of a firearm or imitation firearm by one or more of those involved in robbery.

8. An offence under section 1 of the Protection of Children Act 1978 (indecent images of children).

9. An offence under section 56 of the Terrorism Act 2000 (directing terrorist organisation).

10. An offence under section 57 of that Act (possession of article for terrorist purposes).

11. An offence under section 59 of that Act (inciting terrorism overseas) if the offender is liable on conviction on indictment to imprisonment for life.

12. An offence under section 47 of the Anti-terrorism, Crime and Security Act 2001 (use etc. of nuclear weapons).

13. An offence under section 50 of that Act (assisting or inducing certain weapons-related acts overseas).

14. An offence under section 113 of that Act (use of noxious substance or thing to cause harm or intimidate).

15. An offence under section 1 of the Sexual Offences Act 2003 (rape).

16. An offence under section 2 of that Act (assault by penetration).

17. An offence under section 4 of that Act (causing a person to engage in sexual activity without consent) if the offender is liable on conviction on indictment to imprisonment for life.

18. An offence under section 5 of that Act (rape of a child under 13).

19. An offence under section 6 of that Act (assault of a child under 13 by penetration).

20. An offence under section 7 of that Act (sexual assault of a child under 13).

21. An offence under section 8 of that Act (causing or inciting a child under 13 to engage in sexual activity).

22. An offence under section 9 of that Act (sexual activity with a child).

23. An offence under section 10 of that Act (causing or inciting a child to engage in sexual activity).

24. An offence under section 11 of that Act (engaging in sexual activity in the presence of a child).

25. An offence under section 12 of that Act (causing a child to watch a sexual act).

26. An offence under section 14 of that Act (arranging or facilitating commission of a child sex offence).

27. An offence under section 15 of that Act (meeting a child following sexual grooming etc.).

28. An offence under section 25 of that Act (sexual activity with a child family member) if the offender is aged 18 or over at the time of the offence.

29. An offence under section 26 of that Act (inciting a child family member to engage in sexual activity) if the offender is aged 18 or over at the time of the offence.

30. An offence under section 30 of that Act (sexual activity with a person with a mental disorder impeding choice) if the offender is liable on conviction on indictment to imprisonment for life.

31. An offence under section 31 of that Act (causing or inciting a person with a mental disorder to engage in sexual activity) if the offender is liable on conviction on indictment to imprisonment for life.

32. An offence under section 34 of that Act (inducement, threat or deception to procure sexual activity with a person with a mental disorder) if the offender is liable on conviction on indictment to imprisonment for life.

33. An offence under section 35 of that Act (causing a person with a mental disorder to engage in or agree to engage in sexual activity by inducement etc.) if the offender is liable on conviction on indictment to imprisonment for life.

34. An offence under section 47 of that Act (paying for sexual services of a child) against a person aged under 16.

35. An offence under section 48 of that Act (causing or inciting child prostitution or pornography).

36. An offence under section 49 of that Act (controlling a child prostitute or a child involved in pornography).

37. An offence under section 50 of that Act (arranging or facilitating child prostitution or pornography).

38. An offence under section 62 of that Act (committing an offence with intent to commit a sexual offence) if the offender is liable on conviction on indictment to imprisonment for life.

39. An offence under section 5 of the Domestic Violence, Crime and Victims Act 2004 (causing or allowing the death of a child or vulnerable adult).

40. An offence under section 5 of the Terrorism Act 2006 (preparation of terrorist acts).

41. An offence under section 9 of that Act (making or possession of radioactive device or materials).

42. An offence under section 10 of that Act (misuse of radioactive devices or material and misuse and damage of facilities).

43. An offence under section 11 of that Act (terrorist threats relating to radioactive devices, materials or facilities).

44. (1) An attempt to commit an offence specified in the preceding paragraphs of this Part of this Schedule ("a listed offence") or murder.

    (2) Conspiracy to commit a listed offence or murder.

    (3) Incitement to commit a listed offence or murder.

    (4) An offence under Part 2 of the Serious Crime Act 2007 in relation to which a listed offence or murder is the offence (or one of the offences) which the person intended or believed would be committed.

    (5) Aiding, abetting, counselling or procuring the commission of a listed offence.

45. Murder.

46. Any offence that—

    (a) was abolished (with or without savings) before the coming into force of this Schedule, and

    (b) would, if committed on the day on which the offender was convicted of that offence have constituted an offence specified in Part 1 of this Schedule.

47. An offence under section 70 of the Army Act 1955, section 70 of the Air Force Act 1955 or section 42 of the Naval Discipline Act 1957 as respects which the corresponding civil offence (within the meaning of the Act in question) is an offence specified in Part 1 or 2 of this Schedule.

48. An offence under section 42 of the Armed Forces Act 2006 as respects which the corresponding offence under the law of England and Wales (within the meaning given by that section) is an offence specified in Part 1 or 2 of this Schedule.

49. An offence for which the person was convicted in Scotland, Northern Ireland or a member State other than the United Kingdom and which, if committed in England and Wales at the time of the conviction, would have constituted an offence specified in Part 1 or 2 of this Schedule.

Specified Offences—Young Offenders

CRIMINAL JUSTICE ACT 2003 ss.226B, 228

References: Current Sentencing Practice E5; Archbold 5–499

Detention for life

If an offender aged under 18 on the date of conviction is convicted of a "specified offence" committed on or after April 4, 2005, and the court considers that there is a significant risk to members of the public of serious harm occasioned by the commission by him of further specified offences, the court **must** impose a sentence of detention for life if the offence is punishable with detention for life and the court considers that the seriousness of the offence, or of the offence and one or more offences associated with it, is such as "to justify the imposition of a sentence of detention for life."

For specified offences, see p.257.

Serious harm means "death or serious personal injury, whether physical or psychological".

If the offender is convicted by a youth court or magistrates' court, and it appears to the court that the criteria for the imposition of a sentence of detention for life or an extended sentence of detention would be met, the court must commit the offender to the Crown Court. (See **Committal for Sentence**.)

The sentence of detention for public protection has been abolished.

A court which imposes a sentence of detention for life must fix a minimum term in accordance with the P.C.C.(S.)A. s.82A. The offender may not be released until he has served the minimum term. An offender sentenced to detention for life will remain on licence for the rest of his life.

Extended sentence of detention

The court may impose an extended sentence of detention on a person convicted of any specified offence if the court considers that there is a significant risk to members of the public of serious harm occasioned by the commission by him of further specified offences.

An extended sentence may be imposed whenever the offence was committed, and whether before or after April 4, 2005.

An extended sentence of detention may be imposed only if the appropriate custodial term would be at least four years. *The fact that the offender had been convicted of an offence listed in the Criminal Justice Act 2003 Sch.15B before committing the latest offence is not a qualifying condition for an extended sentence of detention.*

An extended sentence of detention consists of two components: the "appropriate custodial term" and "the extension period". The combined length of the two components must not exceed the maximum sentence for the offence **in the case of a person aged 18 or over.**

The *appropriate custodial term* is the determinate custodial sentence which would have been imposed if the case had not required an extended sentence. In determining this term, the court must comply with the general provisions governing the use of imprisonment, in particular s.153(2), which requires that the custodial term must be the "shortest term" that in the opinion of the court is commensurate with the seriousness of the offence or the combination of the offence and one or more offences associated with it. The custodial term may not be increased beyond what is the shortest term which would be commensurate with the offence, on account of the offender's dangerousness.

If the offender is to be sentenced for more than one specified offence, the appropriate custodial term may not be made up of consecutive terms, each of less than four years but amounting to four years in aggregate, but the sentencer may impose a single term of four years for any one of the offences (subject to the maximum term for that offence) to reflect the seriousness of all of the associated offences for which the offender is being sentenced on that occasion, even though a term of four years would not be commensurate with the seriousness of the particular offence for which it is imposed.

The *extension period* is a period of licence which is "of such length as the court considers necessary for the purpose of protecting members of the public from serious harm occasioned by the commission by him of further specified offences". It must not be more than **five years** in the case of a specified violent offence or **eight years** in the case of a specified sexual offence.

When the Offender Rehabilitation Act 2014 s.8 is in force, there will be a requirement that the extended licence period be for a minimum period of one year.

An offender serving an extended sentence will be released on licence automatically after he has served **two thirds of the appropriate custodial term**, unless the appropriate custodial term is 10 years or more or the offence or one of the offences for which the sentence is imposed is listed in Schedule 15B, Parts 1 to 3. In these cases the offender will not be released unless the Parole Board has directed his release on the ground that it is no longer necessary for the protection of the public that he should be confined, or he has served the whole of the appropriate custodial term and has not been released on licence and recalled.

If an offender qualifies for a hospital order under the Mental Health Act 1983 s.37, the court may make such an order even though the offender otherwise qualifies for a sentence of detention for life or an extended sentence of detention.

For the Criminal Justice Act 2003 Sch.15B, see **Specified Offences— Adults Offenders**.

Surcharge Order

CRIMINAL JUSTICE ACT 2003 s.161A

References: Current Sentencing Practice J17; Archbold 5–1298

Where a court deals with an offender for an offence committed **on or after April 1, 2007, and before October 1, 2012,** by means of a fine (whether or not any other sentence is imposed), the court must order the offender to pay a surcharge of £15. The obligation to make a surcharge order does not apply were the court deals with the offender by means of a compensation order alone, without a fine.

If the court considers that it would be appropriate to make a compensation order in addition to a fine, but that the offender has insufficient means to pay both the surcharge and the appropriate compensation, the court must reduce the surcharge accordingly.

A court may reduce the amount of the fine if it finds that the offender has insufficient means to pay both the appropriate fine and the surcharge.

Offences committed on or after October 1, 2012

These provisions do not apply where a court deals with an offender for more than one offence, and at least one of the offences was committed before October 1, 2012.

The court must make a surcharge in the appropriate amount:

Offences all committed by offender aged under 18 (irrespective of age on date of conviction):

Conditional discharge	£10
Fine	£15
Youth rehabilitation order	£15
Referral order	£15
Community order	£15
Suspended sentence	£20
Custodial sentence imposed by Crown Court	£20
Custodial sentence imposed by magistrates' court or youth court	*no surcharge*

If the court imposes more than one form of sentence, the highest surcharge order applies.

Offences all committed by offender committing when aged over 18:

Conditional discharge	£15
Fine	10 per cent of the value of the fine, rounded up or down to the nearest pound, which must be no less than £20 and no more than £120
Community order	£60
Suspended sentence, where the sentence of imprisonment or detention in a young offender institution is for a period of 6 months or less	£80
Suspended sentence, where the sentence of imprisonment or detention in a young offender institution is for a determinate period of more than 6 months	£100
A sentence of imprisonment or detention in a young offender institution imposed by the Crown Court for a determinate period of up to and including 6 months	£80
A sentence of imprisonment or detention in a young offender institution imposed by the Crown Court for a determinate period of more than 6 months and up to and including 24 months	£100
A sentence of imprisonment or detention in a young offender institution for a determinate period exceeding 24 months	£120
Sentence of imprisonment or detention in a young offender institution imposed by magistrates' court	*no surcharge*
A sentence of imprisonment or custody for life	£120

If the court imposes more than one form of sentence, the highest surcharge order applies.

Offences, some committed when offender under 18 and some when offender over 18

Conditional discharge	£10
Fine	£15
Youth rehabilitation order	£15
Referral order	£15
Community order	£15
Suspended sentence	£20
Custodial sentence imposed by Crown Court	£20
Custodial sentence imposed by magistrates' court or youth court	*no surcharge*

If the court imposes more than one form of sentence, the highest surcharge order applies.

Offences committed by person who is not an individual

Conditional discharge	£15
Fine	10 per cent of the value of the fine, rounded up or down to the nearest pound, which must be no less than £20 and no more than £120

Offence(s) committed on or after September 1, 2014

These provisions do not apply where a court deals with an offender for more than one offence, at least one of which was committed before September 1, 2014: S.I. 2014 No. 2120 art.3.

Note: magistrates' courts imposing custodial sentences are now required to impose a surcharge order.

The court must make a surcharge in the appropriate amount:

Offences all committed by offender aged under 18 (irrespective of age on date of conviction):

Conditional discharge	£10
Fine	£15
Youth rehabilitation order	£15

Referral order	£15
Community order	£15
Suspended sentence	£20
Custodial sentence	£20

Offences all committed by offender committing when aged over 18:

Conditional discharge	£15
Fine	10 per cent of the value of the fine, rounded up or down to the nearest pound, which must be no less than £20 and no more than £120
Community order	£60
Suspended sentence, where the sentence of imprisonment or detention in a young offender institution is for a period of 6 months or less	£80
Suspended sentence, where the sentence of imprisonment or detention in a young offender institution is for a determinate period of more than 6 months	£100
A sentence of imprisonment or detention in a young offender institution for a determinate period of up to and including 6 months	£80
A sentence of imprisonment or detention in a young offender institution for a determinate period of more than 6 months and up to and including 24 months	£100
A sentence of imprisonment or detention in a young offender institution for a determinate period exceeding 24 months	£120
A sentence of imprisonment or custody for life	£120

Offences, some committed when offender under 18 and some when offender over 18:

Conditional discharge	£10
Fine	£15
Youth rehabilitation order	£15
Referral order	£15

Community order	£15
Suspended sentence	£20
Custodial sentence	£20

Surcharge orders are enforced in accordance with the Administration of Justice Act 1970 Sch.9. ***The Crown Court does not fix a default term when making a surcharge order.***

Suspended Sentence Order

CRIMINAL JUSTICE ACT 2003 ss.189–193

References: Current Sentencing Practice A13A; Archbold 5–547

Note: the sections of the Criminal Justice Act 2003 mentioned above are subject to temporary modifications.

A court which passes a sentence of imprisonment or detention in a young offender institution for a term of at least 14 days but **not more than two years** may order that the sentence of imprisonment is not to take effect unless the offender commits another offence during the period specified in the order. The court must fix the "operational period". The operational period must be at least six months and not more than two years. If the offender commits an offence during the operational period, he will be liable to be ordered to serve the sentence.

In making a suspended sentence order the court **may** order the offender to comply with such requirements (known as "community requirements") as may be specified during the "supervision period". The supervision period must be at least six months and not more than two years; the supervision period may not extend beyond the operational period, but the operational period may extend beyond the end of the supervision period. If the court passes a suspended sentence, it may not impose a community sentence in respect of that offence or any other offence for which the offender is sentenced by the court.

The community requirements which may be included in a suspended sentence order are all of those which may be included in a community order, subject to the same conditions as apply to a community order. (See **Community Order—Criminal Justice Act 2003—Requirements**.)

If a court imposes two sentences to be served consecutively, the power to suspend the sentence is available only if the aggregate term does not exceed two years.

A suspended sentence order which includes one or more community requirements may provide for periodic review of the order by the court which made the order, except where the requirement is a drug rehabilitation requirement, in which case periodic reviews are provided for in the provisions governing the requirement itself.

Where a suspended sentence order is made by the Crown Court, the Crown Court should consider whether to direct that any failure to comply with a community requirement of the sentence should be dealt with by the magistrates' court. If no such direction is given, any alleged breach of the community requirement will be brought before the Crown Court.

Breach of suspended sentence order (Sch.12)

A "breach" of a suspended sentence order may occur either by a failure to comply with a community requirement during the supervision period, or by the commission of an offence during the operational period. *As these two periods may be different in any particular case, it will be important to ensure that the relevant event took place during the relevant period.*

Where it is alleged that an offender has *failed to comply with a community requirement*, the offender will be brought before the appropriate court. If it is proved to the satisfaction of the court that the offender has failed to comply with any of the community requirements of the order without reasonable excuse, the court may order the sentence to take effect with the original term unaltered, or may order the sentence to take effect with the term reduced. Alternatively the court may impose more onerous community requirements, extend either the supervision period or the operational period, or impose a *fine not exceeding £2,500.* (A fine may not be imposed if the breach took place before December 3, 2012.) The operational period may not be extended beyond the end of a period of two years beginning on the date the original order was made.

The court **must order the sentence to take effect**, either in its original form or with a reduction of the term of the sentence, unless it would be **"unjust to do so in all the circumstances"**. If the court considers that it would be unjust to do so, it must state its reasons. If the court does not order the suspended sentence to take effect, it must take one of the other courses provided.

If the offender is **convicted of an offence** committed during the operational period of a suspended sentence, he may be dealt with in respect of the suspended sentence by a magistrates' court only if the suspended sentence was passed by a magistrates' court. If the suspended sentence was passed by the Crown Court and the offender is convicted by a magistrates' court of the later offence, the magistrates' court may commit him to the Crown Court to be dealt with. If the magistrates' court does not commit the offender to the Crown Court, it must notify the Crown Court, and the Crown Court may issue process to secure his appearance before the Crown Court.

If the offender is convicted by the Crown Court of an offence committed during the operational period of a suspended sentence, the Crown Court may deal with the suspended sentence whether the suspended sentence was passed by the Crown Court or by a magistrates' court.

It is not necessary that the later offence should be punishable with imprisonment.

Where the court has power to deal with the suspended sentence, the court may order the sentence to take effect with the original term unaltered, order the sentence to take effect with the term reduced, extend the operational period or impose a fine not exceeding £2,500. The operational period may not be extended beyond the end of a period of two years beginning on the date the original order was made. If the suspended sentence includes one or more community requirements the court may impose more onerous community requirements, or extend the supervision period. *The court must order the sentence to take effect, either in its original form or with a reduction of the term of the sentence, unless it would be "unjust to do so in all the circumstances", having regard in particular to the extent to which the offender has complied with the community requirements and the facts of the latest offence.* If the court considers that it would be unjust to order the sentence to take effect, it must state its reasons. If the court does not order the suspended sentence to take effect, it must take one of the other courses provided.

The court may not revoke the order and impose a custodial sentence of greater length than the sentence which was suspended.

Where an offender who is subject to a suspended sentence appears for sentence for an offence committed before the suspended sentence was imposed, the court has no power to order the suspended sentence to take effect, to impose more onerous requirements or extend the operational period, but may cancel the community requirement of the suspended sentence order on the application of the offender or responsible officer.

Terrorist Connected Offences

COUNTER-TERRORISM ACT 2008 s.30

References: Current Sentencing Practice H 14; Archbold 25–213

Where a person is convicted of an offence listed in Sch.2 to the Counter-Terrorism Act 2008 committed **on or after June 18, 2009** and it appears to the court that the offence has or may have a terrorist connection, the court must determine whether the offence has a terrorist connection. The court may hear evidence for the purpose of determining whether the offence has a terrorist connection, and must take account of any representations made by the prosecution and defence, and any other matter relevant for the purposes of sentence. *If the court determines that the offence has a terrorist connection, the court* **must** *treat that fact as an aggravating factor and* **must** *state in open court that the offence was so aggravated.*

For the offences listed in Sch.2, see p.264.

An "ancillary offence" is an offence of aiding, abetting, counselling or procuring the commission of the offence, an offence under Pt 2 of the Serious Crime Act 2007 (ch.27) in relation to the offence, or attempting or conspiring to commit the offence.

An offence has a terrorist connection if the offence is, or takes place in the course of, an act of terrorism, or is committed for the purposes of terrorism.

"Terrorism" means the use or threat of action where the action: (a) involves *serious violence* against a person; (b) involves *serious damage* to property; (c) *endangers a person's life*, other than that of the person committing the action; (d) creates a *serious risk to the health or safety* of the public or a section of the public; or (e) is designed seriously to interfere with or *seriously to disrupt an electronic system*, and the use or threat is designed to *influence the government or to intimidate the public* or a section of the public, and the use or threat is made for the purpose of *advancing a political, religious, racial or ideological cause.*

An action which: (a) involves serious violence against a person; (b) involves serious damage to property; (c) endangers a person's life, other than that of the person committing the action; (d) creates a serious risk to the health or safety of the public or a section of the public; or (e) is designed seriously to interfere with or seriously to disrupt an electronic system, and involves the *use of firearms or explosives* is terrorism whether or not the use or is designed to influence the government or to intimidate the public or a section of the public.

"Action" includes action outside the United Kingdom, a reference to "any person or to property" is a reference to any person, or to property, wherever situated, a reference to "the public" includes a reference to the public of a country other than the United Kingdom, and "the government" means the government of the United Kingdom, of a part of the United Kingdom or of a country other than the United Kingdom. A reference to "action taken for the purposes of terrorism" includes a reference to action *taken for the benefit of a proscribed organisation.*

A person in respect of whom the court makes a determination that the offences of which he has been convicted may become liable to notification requirements. If a person becomes liable to notification requirements, he may appeal against the determination that the offence has a terrorist connection as if that determination were a sentence.

Notification requirements apply to a person who was **16 or over when the offence was committed** and who has been sentenced to an indeterminate sentence, or a term of imprisonment, detention in a young offender institution, detention under the Powers of Criminal Courts (Sentencing) Act 2000 s.91, or a detention and training order for a term of 12 months or more, or who has been sentenced to a hospital order on conviction of an offence punishable with 12 months or more, or found not guilty by reason of insanity or found to be under a disability having done the act charged. *No express provision is made for suspended sentence orders.*

Notification requirements apply also to persons convicted of offences contrary to the Terrorism Act 2000, the Anti-terrorism, Crime and Security Act 2001, and the Terrorism Act 2006

The periods for which the notification requirements apply are:

Offender aged 18 *at the time of conviction*

and sentenced to an indeterminate sentence or a
determinate sentence of 10 years or more   **30 years**

Offender aged 18 *at the time of conviction*

and sentenced to a term of at least 5 years but less
than 10 years   **15 years**

All other cases   **10 years**

The notification period begins on the day the person is dealt with for the offence, but in determining whether it has expired, any period when the person was in custody on remand or serving a sentence or imprisonment or detention, or detained in a hospital, or under the Immigration Acts is disregarded.

The sentencing court is not required to make any order or give any explanation of a notification requirement.

Time in Custody on Remand—Criminal Justice Act 2003

CRIMINAL JUSTICE ACT 2003 s.240ZA

References: Current Sentencing Practice A6A, Archbold 5–639

These provisions apply to offenders serving a term of imprisonment, an extended sentence of imprisonment or detention in a young offender institution, a determinate sentence of detention in a young offender institution, a determinate sentence of detention under the Powers of Criminal Courts (Sentencing) Act 2000 s.91, or an extended sentence of detention. *They do not apply to offenders serving sentences of life imprisonment, custody for life, detention for life or detention and training orders.*

These provisions apply to any person sentenced on or after December 3, 2012, irrespective of the date on which the offence was committed.

If the offender has been remanded in custody for the offence or a related offence, the number of days for which the offender was remanded in custody count as time served as part of the sentence, unless on any day the offender was detained in connection with any other matter. A day may be counted in relation to only one sentence, and only once in relation to that sentence.

It is not necessary for the sentencing court to make any order in relation to time spent in custody on remand.

A related offence is an offence with which the offender was charged and which was founded on the same facts or evidence as the offence for which the sentence was imposed.

A day spent in custody in connection with any other matter does not include a day spent in custody on remand in connection with another offence.

If the offender has been extradited the court must specify in open court the number of days for which the offender was kept in custody while awaiting extradition. Such days are treated as counting as time served as part of the sentence. *The court has no discretion to disallow any days spent in custody while awaiting extradition.*

Time Spent on Remand on Bail Subject to Qualifying Curfew Condition

CRIMINAL JUSTICE ACT s.240A

References: Current Sentencing Practice A6B; Archbold 5–645

These provisions apply where a court sentences an offender to a term of imprisonment, an extended sentence of imprisonment, a determinate sentence of detention in a young offender institution or an extended sentence of detention in a young offender institution, a determinate sentence of detention under s.91 of the P.C.C.(S.)A. 2000, an extended sentence of detention, and the offender was remanded on bail by a court in course of or in connection with proceedings for the offence, or any related offence. The section does not apply to a detention and training order or the minimum term of an indeterminate sentence but the court should make an appropriate allowance in determining the length of the detention and training order or minimum term.

These provisions apply to offences committed before April 4, 2005, as well as to offences committed on or after that date.

If the offender is subject to a suspended sentence or suspended sentence order, the provisions apply to the court which activates the sentence, not the court which imposes the sentence.

If the offender's bail was subject to a **qualifying curfew condition and an electronic monitoring condition,** the court must direct that the credit period is to count as time served by the offender as part of the sentence. The "credit period" is the number of days represented by half of the sum of the day on which the offender's bail was first subject to conditions that would have been relevant conditions, and the number of other days on which the offender's bail was subject to those conditions (excluding the last day if the offender spends part of that day in custody), rounded up to the nearest whole number.

Any day on which the offender was subject to electronic monitoring to secure his compliance with a curfew requirement, or is on temporary release from custody, is not counted. Any day on which the offender has broken either the curfew condition or the electronic monitoring condition is not counted.

A day of the credit period counts as time served in relation to only one sentence and only once in relation to that sentence.

An "**electronic monitoring condition**" is any electronic monitoring requirement imposed under the Bail Act 1976 for the purpose of securing the electronic monitoring of a person's compliance with a qualifying curfew condition.

A "**qualifying curfew condition**" means a condition of bail which requires the person granted bail to remain at one or more specified places *for a total of not less than nine hours in any given day*.

"Related offence" means an offence, other than the offence for which the sentence is imposed, with which the offender was charged and *the charge for which was founded on the same facts or evidence* as the offence for which the sentence is imposed.

Travel Restriction Order

CRIMINAL JUSTICE AND POLICE ACT 2001 S.33

References: Current Sentencing Practice H9–1; Archbold 5–1141

Where a court convicts an offender of a drug trafficking offence **as defined in s.34 of the Act committed on or after April 1, 2002,** and determines that it would be appropriate to impose a sentence of imprisonment of four years or more, the court must consider whether it would be appropriate to make a travel restriction order in relation to the offender; if the court determines that it would be appropriate to do so, the court must make such travel restriction order as it thinks suitable in all the circumstances. If the court determines that it is not appropriate to make a travel restriction order, it must state its reasons for not making one.

The following offences are "drug trafficking offences" for this purpose: offences under the Misuse of Drugs Act 1971 ss.4(2), 4(3), 19 and 20; offences under the Customs and Excise Management Act 1979 ss.50(2), 50(3), 68(2), 170 (in relation to prohibited drugs), and attempts, conspiracies or incitements in relation to these offences.

Possession with intent to supply, and money laundering offences, are not included.

A travel restriction order must be for at least two years.

A travel restriction order prohibits the offender from leaving the United Kingdom at any time during the period beginning with his release from custody and continuing to the end of the period specified by the court. *A travel restriction order may contain a direction to the offender to deliver up to the court any UK passport held by him.*

A court which has made a travel restriction order may revoke or suspend the order on an application made by the offender at any time which after the end of the minimum period, and not less than three months after the making of any previous application for the revocation of the prohibition.

The minimum period in the case of an order for four years or less is a period of two years, in the case of an order for more than four years but less than 10 years is a period of four years, and in any other case is a period of five years.

A court must not revoke a travel restriction order unless it considers that it is appropriate to do so in all the circumstances of the case and having regard, in particular the offender's character, his conduct since the making of the order, and the offences of which he was convicted on the occasion on which the order was made.

A court must not suspend a travel restriction order for any period unless it is satisfied that there are exceptional circumstances that justify the suspension on compassionate grounds. A court must not suspend a travel restriction order unless it considers that it is appropriate to do so in all the circumstances of the case and having regard, in particular the offender's character, his conduct since the making of the order, the offences of which he was convicted on the occasion on which the order was made and any other circumstances of the case that the court considers relevant.

Unfit to Plead (Crown Court)

CRIMINAL PROCEDURE (INSANITY) ACT 1964 s.5

References: Archbold 4–239

Where findings are recorded that a person is under a disability and *that he did the act or made the omission charged against him*, the court may make a hospital order (with or without a restriction order), a supervision order under the Criminal Procedure (Insanity) Act 1964 Sch.1A, or an order for absolute discharge.

The court must not make a supervision order unless it is satisfied that, having regard to all the circumstances of the case, the making of such an order is the most suitable means of dealing with the person, that the supervising officer intended to be specified in the order is willing to undertake the supervision, and that arrangements have been made for the treatment intended to be specified in the order.

An order for absolute discharge may be made if the court considers that such an order would be most suitable in all the circumstances of the case.

Where the offence to which the findings relate is an offence for which the sentence is fixed by law, and the court has power to make a hospital order, the court must make a hospital order with a restriction order.

Before making a supervision order, the court must explain in ordinary language the effect of the order and that a magistrates' court has power to review the order on the application either of the supervised person or of the supervising officer.

A supervision order may include a requirement that the supervised person shall, during the whole or part of the period specified in the order, submit to treatment by or under the direction of a registered medical practitioner with a view to the improvement of his mental condition. A treatment requirement may be imposed only if the court is satisfied on the written or oral evidence of two or more registered medical practitioners that the mental condition of the supervised person is such as requires and may be susceptible to treatment, but is not such as to warrant the making of a hospital order. The treatment required may be treatment as a non-resident patient at a specified institution or place and treatment by or under the direction of a specified registered medical practitioner.

A supervision order may include requirements as to the residence of the supervised person.

Youth Rehabilitation Order

CRIMINAL JUSTICE AND IMMIGRATION ACT 2008 s.1

References: Archbold 5–314

Where a person **under 18** is convicted of an offence, the court may make a youth rehabilitation order containing specified requirements. *A youth rehabilitation order may be made only if the court is of the opinion that the offence or the combination of the offence and one or more offences associated with it was serious enough to warrant a youth rehabilitation order, the particular requirements forming part of the order are the most suitable for the offender and the restrictions on liberty imposed by the order are commensurate with the seriousness of the offence or the combination of the offence and one or more offences associated with it.*

A youth rehabilitation order may not be made where the court is required to impose a mandatory custodial sentence.

Before making a youth rehabilitation order, the court must obtain and consider information about the offender's family circumstances and the likely effect of the order on those circumstances. Before making an order with two or more requirements, or two or more orders in respect of associated offences, the court must consider whether the requirements are compatible with each other. The requirements must so far as is practicable avoid conflict with the offender's religious beliefs, avoid any interference with the times at which the offender normally works or attends any school or educational establishment, and avoid any conflict with the requirements of any other youth rehabilitation order to which the offender is subject.

A youth rehabilitation order takes effect on the day on which it is made. If the offender is subject to a detention and training order, the court may order the youth rehabilitation order to take effect when the offender is released from custody under supervision, or at the expiry of the term of the detention and training order.

A youth rehabilitation order must specify a date, not more than three years after the date on which the order takes effect, by which all the requirements in it must have been complied with. An order which imposes two or more different requirements may also specify a date or dates in relation to compliance with any one or more of them; the last such date must be the date by which all the requirements must be satisfied. In the case of a youth rehabilitation order with intensive supervision and surveillance, the date specified must not be earlier than six months after the date on which the order takes effect.

Where the Crown Court makes a youth rehabilitation order, it may give a direction that further proceedings relating to the order should be in a youth court or other magistrates' court.

The following requirements may be included in a youth rehabilitation order:

Activity requirement. An activity requirement is a requirement that the offender must participate in specified activities at a specified place or places, or participate in one or more residential exercises for a continuous period or periods of the number or numbers of days to be specified in the order, or engage in activities in accordance with instructions of the responsible officer on the number of days specified in the order. The total number of days specified in an activity requirement must not in aggregate exceed 90.

Supervision requirement. A supervision requirement is a requirement that the offender must attend appointments with the responsible officer or another person determined by the responsible officer, at such times and places as may be determined by the responsible officer.

Unpaid work requirement. An unpaid work requirement is a requirement that the offender must perform unpaid work. The number of hours or work must be not less than 40, and not more than 240. **An unpaid work requirement may be made only if the offender is 16 or 17 at the time of conviction**.

A court may not impose an unpaid work requirement unless after hearing (if the court thinks necessary) an appropriate officer, the court is satisfied that the offender is a suitable person to perform work under such a requirement, and the court is satisfied that provision for the offender to work under such a requirement can be made existing local arrangements.

The work must be performed at such times as the responsible officer may specify in instructions. The work must be performed during the period of 12 months beginning with the day on which the order takes effect. A youth rehabilitation order imposing an unpaid work requirement remains in force until the offender has worked under it for the number of hours specified in it, unless the order is revoked.

Programme requirement. A programme requirement is a requirement that the offender must participate in a systematic programme of activities specified in the order at a place or places so specified on such number of days as may be so specified. A programme requirement may require the offender to reside at any place specified in the order for any period so specified if it is necessary for the offender to reside there for that period in order to participate in the programme.

A court may not include a programme requirement in a youth rehabilitation order unless the programme has been recommended to the court by a member of a youth offending team, an officer of a local probation board, or an officer of a provider of probation services, as being suitable for the offender, and the court is satisfied that the programme is available at the place or places proposed to be specified.

A court may not include a programme requirement in a youth rehabilitation order if compliance with that requirement would involve the **co-operation of a person other than the offender** and the offender's responsible officer, **unless that other person consents to its inclusion**.

Attendance centre requirement. An attendance centre requirement is a requirement that the offender must attend at an attendance centre specified in the order for such number of hours as may be so specified.

If the offender is **aged 16 or over** at the time of conviction, the aggregate number of hours for which the offender may be required to attend at an attendance centre must be **not less than 12, and not more than 36**.

If the offender is **aged 14 or over but under 16** at the time of conviction, the aggregate number of hours for which the offender may be required to attend at an attendance centre must **be not less than 12, and not more than 24**.

If the offender is aged **under 14** at the time of conviction, the aggregate number of hours for which the offender may be required to attend at an attendance centre **must not be more than 12**.

A court may not include an attendance centre requirement in a youth rehabilitation order unless it has been notified by the Secretary of State that an attendance centre is available for persons of the offender's description, and provision can be made at the centre for the offender. The court must be satisfied that the attendance centre proposed is reasonably accessible to the offender, having regard to the means of access available to the offender and any other circumstances.

Prohibited activity requirement. A prohibited activity requirement is a requirement that the offender must refrain from participating in activities specified in the order, on a day or days specified in the during a period specified in the order.

A court may not include a prohibited activity requirement in a youth rehabilitation order unless it has consulted a member of a youth offending team, an officer of a local probation board, or an officer of a provider of probation services.

The requirements that may be included in a youth rehabilitation order include a requirement that the offender does not possess, use or carry a firearm.

Curfew requirement. A curfew requirement is a requirement that the offender must remain, for periods specified in the order, at a place so specified. A curfew requirement may specify different places or different periods for different days, but may not specify periods which amount to less than two hours or more than 16 hours (12 hours if the offence was committed before December 3, 2012) in any day.

A curfew requirement may not specify periods which fall outside the period of 12 months (six months if the offence was committed before December 3, 2012) beginning with the day on which the requirement first takes effect.

Before making a youth rehabilitation order imposing a curfew requirement, the court must obtain and consider information about the place proposed to be specified in the order (including information as to the attitude of persons likely to be affected by the enforced presence there of the offender).

Where a curfew requirement is made, **the order must also include an electronic monitoring requirement**, unless the court considers it inappropriate for the order to include an electronic monitoring requirement, or it will not be practicable to secure that the monitoring takes place, without the consent of some person other than the offender, and that person does not consent to the inclusion of the electronic monitoring requirement.

Exclusion requirement. An exclusion requirement is a provision prohibiting the offender from entering a place or area specified in the order for a period so specified, which **must not exceed three months**.

An exclusion requirement may provide for the prohibition to operate only during the periods specified in the order, and may specify different places for different periods or days.

Where an exclusion requirement is made, **the order must also include an electronic monitoring requirement**, unless the court considers it inappropriate for the order to include an electronic monitoring requirement, or it will not be practicable to secure that the monitoring takes place, without the consent of some person other than the offender, and that person does not consent to the inclusion of the electronic monitoring requirement.

Residence requirement. A residence requirement is a requirement that, during the period specified in the order, the offender must reside with an individual specified in the order, or at a place specified in the order.

A residence requirement that the offender reside with an individual may not be made unless that individual has consented to the requirement.

A requirement that the offender reside at a specified place may not be made unless the offender was aged 16 or over at the time of conviction. A requirement that the offender reside at a specified place may provide that the offender may reside, with the prior approval of the responsible officer, at a place other than that specified in the order.

Before making a requirement that the offender reside at a specified place, the court must consider the home surroundings of the offender. The court may not specify a hostel or other institution as the place where an offender must reside except on the recommendation of a member of a youth offending team, an officer of a local probation board, an officer of a provider of probation services, or a social worker of a local authority.

Local authority residence requirement. A local authority residence requirement is a requirement that, during the period specified in the order, the offender must reside in accommodation provided by or on behalf of a local authority specified in the order for the purposes of the requirement. The period for which the offender must reside in local authority accommodation **must not be longer than 6 months, and must not include any period after the offender has reached the age of 18**.

An order containing a local authority residence requirement may also stipulate that the offender is not to reside with a person specified in the order.

A court may not make a local authority residence requirement unless it is satisfied that the behaviour which constituted the offence was due to a significant extent to the circumstances in which the offender was living, and that the imposition of that requirement will assist in the offender's rehabilitation.

A court may not include a local authority residence requirement in a youth rehabilitation order unless it has consulted a parent or guardian of the offender (unless it is impracticable to consult such a person), and the local authority which is to receive the offender.

A local authority residence requirement may not be made unless the offender was **legally represented** at the relevant time in court, or a right to representation funded by the Legal Services Commission for the purposes of the proceedings was withdrawn because of the offender's conduct, or the offender refused or failed to apply for representation after being informed of the right to apply and having had the opportunity to do so.

A local authority residence requirement must specify, as the local authority which is to receive the offender, the local authority in whose area the offender resides or is to reside.

Mental health treatment requirement. A mental health treatment requirement is a requirement that the offender must submit, during a period or periods specified in the order, to treatment by or under the direction of a registered medical practitioner or a chartered psychologist (or both, for different periods) with a view to the improvement of the offender's mental condition.

The treatment required must be treatment as a resident patient in an independent hospital or care home, or a hospital within the meaning of the Mental Health Act 1983, but not in hospital premises where high security psychiatric services are provided, treatment as a non-resident patient at such institution or place as may be specified in the order, or treatment by or under the direction of such registered medical practitioner or chartered psychologist (or both) as may be so specified. The nature of the treatment is not specified in the order.

A court may not make a mental health treatment requirement unless the court is satisfied that the mental condition of the offender is such as requires and may be susceptible to treatment, but is not such as to warrant the making of a hospital order or guardianship order within the meaning of that Act. The court must be satisfied that arrangements have been or can be made for the treatment intended to be specified in the order (including, where the offender is to be required to submit to treatment as a resident patient, arrangements for the reception of the offender), and **the offender has expressed willingness to comply with the requirement**.

Drug treatment requirement. A drug treatment requirement is a require-ment that the offender must submit, during a period or periods specified in the order, to treatment, by or under the direction of a treatment provider with a view to the reduction or elimination of the offender's dependency on, or propensity to misuse, drugs.

A court may not include a drug treatment requirement in a youth rehabilitation order unless it is *satisfied that the offender is dependent on, or has a propensity to misuse, drugs, and that the offender's dependency or propensity is such as requires and may be susceptible to treatment.*

The treatment required may be treatment as a resident in such institution or place as may be specified in the order, or treatment as a non-resident at such institution or place, and at such intervals, as may be so specified. The nature of the treatment is not specified in the order.

A court must not make a drug treatment requirement unless the court has been notified by the Secretary of State that arrangements for implementing drug treatment requirements are in force in the local justice area in which the offender resides or is to reside, and the court is satisfied that arrangements have been or can be made for the treatment intended to be specified in the order. The requirement must be recommended to the court as suitable for the offender by a member of a youth offending team, an officer of a local probation board or an officer of a provider of probation services, and **the offender must express willingness to comply with the requirement**.

Drug testing requirement. A drug testing requirement is a requirement that the offender must, during the treatment period of a drug treatment requirement, provide samples in accordance with instructions given by the responsible officer or the treatment provider for the purpose of ascertaining whether there is any drug in the offender's body.

A court may not include a drug testing requirement in a youth rehabilitation order unless the court has been notified by the Secretary of State that arrangements for implementing drug testing requirements are in force in the local justice area in which the offender resides or is to reside, the order also imposes a drug treatment requirement, and **the offender has expressed willingness to comply with the requirement**.

A drug testing requirement must specify for each month the minimum number of occasions on which samples are to be provided, and may specify times at which and circumstances in which the responsible officer or treatment provider may require samples to be provided, and descriptions of the samples which may be so required.

A drug testing requirement must provide for the results of tests carried out otherwise than by the responsible officer on samples provided by the offender in pursuance of the requirement to be communicated to the responsible officer.

Intoxicating substance treatment requirement. An intoxicating substance treatment requirement is a requirement that the offender must submit, during a period or periods specified in the order, to treatment, by or under the direction of a specified qualified person with a view to the reduction or elimination of the offender's dependency on or propensity to misuse intoxicating substances.

A court may not include an intoxicating substance treatment requirement in a youth rehabilitation order unless it is satisfied that the offender is dependent on, or has a propensity to misuse, intoxicating substances, and that the offender's dependency or propensity is such as requires and may be susceptible to treatment.

The treatment required must be treatment as a resident in an institution or place specified in the order, or treatment as a non-resident in a specified institution or place, at specified intervals. The nature of the treatment is not specified.

A court may not make an intoxicating substance treatment requirement unless the court is satisfied that arrangements have been or can be made for the treatment intended to be specified in the order, the requirement has been recommended to the court as suitable for the offender by a member of a youth offending team, an officer of a local probation board or an officer of a provider of probation services, and **the offender has expressed willingness to comply with the requirement**.

Education requirement.   An education requirement is a requirement that the offender must comply, during a period or periods specified in the order, with approved education arrangements made for the time being by the offender's parent or guardian, and approved by the local education authority specified in the order.

A court may not include an education requirement in a youth rehabilitation order unless it has consulted the local education authority proposed to be specified in the order with regard to the proposal to include the requirement, and it is satisfied that, in the view of that local education authority, arrangements exist for the offender to receive efficient full-time education suitable to the offender's age, ability, aptitude and special educational needs (if any), and that, having regard to the circumstances of the case, the inclusion of the education requirement is necessary for securing the good conduct of the offender or for preventing the commission of further offences.

Any period specified in a youth rehabilitation order as a period during which an offender must comply with approved education arrangements must not include any period after the offender has ceased to be of compulsory school age.

Electronic monitoring requirement.   An electronic monitoring requirement is a requirement for securing the electronic monitoring of the offender's compliance with other requirements imposed by the order during a period specified in the order or determined by the responsible officer in accordance with the order.

Where it is proposed to make an electronic monitoring requirement, but there is a person (other than the offender) without whose co-operation it will not be practicable to secure that the monitoring takes place, the requirement may not be included in the order without that person's consent.

A youth rehabilitation order which imposes an electronic monitoring requirement must include provision for making a person of a description specified in an order made by the Secretary of State responsible for the monitoring.

A court may not make an electronic monitoring requirement unless the court has been notified by the Secretary of State that arrangements for electronic monitoring of offenders are available in the local justice area proposed to be specified in the order, and in the area in which the relevant place is situated, and is satisfied that the necessary provision can be made under the arrangements currently available.

An electronic monitoring requirement must be made where the court makes either a curfew requirement or an exclusion requirement, unless the court considers it inappropriate for the order to include an electronic monitoring requirement, or it will not be practicable to secure that the monitoring takes place, without the consent of some person other than the offender, and that person does not consent to the inclusion of the electronic monitoring requirement.

Intensive supervision and surveillance. A court may make a youth rehabilitation order with intensive supervision and surveillance if the court is dealing with an offender for an offence which is punishable with imprisonment, and the court is of the opinion that the offence, or the combination of the offence and one or more offences associated with it, was so serious that a custodial sentence would be appropriate (or, if the offender was aged under 12 at the time of conviction, would be appropriate if the offender had been aged 12) in the absence of a power to make a youth rehabilitation order with intensive supervision and surveillance or a youth rehabilitation order with fostering. If the offender was aged under 15 at the time of conviction, the court must also be of the opinion that the offender is a persistent offender.

If the court makes a youth rehabilitation order with intensive supervision and surveillance, the order may include an extended activity requirement of more than 90 but not more than 180 days, and must make a supervision requirement and a curfew requirement with an electronic monitoring requirement, where such a requirement is required. A youth rehabilitation order with intensive supervision and surveillance may include other types of requirement, except a fostering requirement.

Fostering requirement. A court may make a youth rehabilitation order with a fostering requirement if the court is dealing with an offender for an offence which is punishable with imprisonment, and the court is of the opinion that the offence, or the combination of the offence and one or more offences associated with it, was so serious that a custodial sentence would be appropriate (or, if the offender was aged under 12 at the time of conviction, would be appropriate if the offender had been aged 12) in the absence of a power to make a youth rehabilitation order with intensive supervision and surveillance or a youth rehabilitation order with fostering. If the offender was aged under 15 at the time of conviction, the court must also be of the opinion that the offender is a persistent offender.

A fostering requirement may be made only if the court is satisfied that the behaviour which constituted the offence was due to a significant extent to the circumstances in which the offender was living, and that the imposition of a fostering requirement would assist in the offender's rehabilitation. A court may not impose a fostering requirement unless it has consulted the offender's parents or guardians (unless it is impracticable to do so), and it has consulted the local authority which is to place the offender with a local authority foster parent.

A youth rehabilitation order which imposes a fostering requirement must also impose a supervision requirement.

A fostering requirement is a requirement that, for a period specified in the order, the offender must reside with a local authority foster parent.

The period specified must end no later than 12 months beginning with the date on which the requirement first has effect and not include any period after the offender has reached the age of 18.

If at any time during the period of the requirement, the responsible officer notifies the offender that no suitable local authority foster parent is available, and that the responsible officer has applied or proposes to apply for the revocation or amendment of the order, the fostering requirement is, until the determination of the application, to be taken to require the offender to reside in accommodation provided by or on behalf of a local authority.

A court may not include a fostering requirement in a youth rehabilitation order unless the court has been notified by the Secretary of State that arrangements for implementing such a requirement are available in the area of the local authority which is to place the offender with a local authority foster parent.

A fostering requirement may not be made unless the offender was **legally represented** at the relevant time in court, or a right to representation funded by the Legal Services Commission for the purposes of the proceedings was withdrawn because of the offender's conduct, or the offender refused or failed to apply for representation after being informed of the right to apply and having had the opportunity to do so.

A fostering requirement may not be included in a youth rehabilitation order with intensive supervision and surveillance.

Breach of requirement of order

Youth court

If it is proved to the satisfaction of a youth court or magistrates court that an offender subject to a youth rehabilitation order has failed without reasonable excuse to comply with the youth rehabilitation order, the court may deal with the offender by ordering the offender to pay a fine not exceeding £2,500 (except where the failure took place before December 3, 2012); by amending the terms of the order so as to impose any requirement which could have been included in the order when it was made in addition to, or in substitution for any requirement or requirements already imposed by the order; or by dealing with the offender, for the offence in respect of which the order was made, in any way in which the court could have dealt with the offender for that offence.

If the court imposes a new requirement, the period for compliance with the order may be extended by up to six months, unless the period has previously been extended, or unless the order was made before December 3, 2012.

If the order imposes a mental health treatment requirement, a drug treatment requirement, or an intoxicating substance treatment requirement, the offender is not to be treated as having failed to comply with the order on the ground only that the offender had refused to undergo any surgical, electrical or other treatment, if in the opinion of the court, the refusal was reasonable having regard to all the circumstances.

If the court deals with the offender for the offence, the court must take into account the extent to which the offender has complied with the order. The order must be revoked.

If the order does not contain an unpaid work requirement, the court may add an unpaid work requirement with a requirement to perform between

20 and 240 hours' work. The court may not add to an existing youth rehabilitation order an extended activity requirement, or a fostering requirement, if the order does not already impose such a requirement.

If the order imposes a fostering requirement, the court may impose a new fostering requirement ending not later than 18 months from the date on which the original order was made.

If the court is dealing with the offender for the original offence, and the offender has wilfully and persistently failed to comply with a youth rehabilitation order, the court may impose a youth rehabilitation order with intensive supervision and surveillance.

If the order is a youth rehabilitation order with intensive supervision and surveillance, and the offence for which it was imposed was punishable with imprisonment, the court may impose a custodial sentence notwithstanding the general restrictions on imposing discretionary custodial sentences.

If the order is a youth rehabilitation order with intensive supervision and surveillance which was imposed following the breach of an earlier order, and the original offence was not punishable with imprisonment, the court may deal with the offender by making a detention and training order for a term not exceeding 4 months.

Crown Court

If the order made by the Crown Court contains a direction that further proceedings should be in the youth court or magistrates' court, the youth court or magistrates' court may commit the offender in custody or on bail, to be brought or appear before the Crown Court.

Where an offender appears or is brought before the Crown Court and it is proved to the satisfaction of that court that the offender has failed without reasonable excuse to comply with the youth rehabilitation order, the court may order the offender to pay a fine not exceeding £2,500 (except where the failure took place before December 3, 2012); amend the terms of the youth rehabilitation order so as to impose any requirement which could have been included in the order when it was made, in addition to, or in substitution for, any requirement or requirements already imposed by the order; or deal with the offender, for the offence in respect of which the order was made, in any way in which the Crown Court could have dealt with the offender for that offence.

If the court imposes a new requirement, the period for compliance with the order may be extended by up to six months, unless the period has previously been extended, or unless the order was made before December 3, 2012.

If the order imposes a mental health treatment requirement, a drug treatment requirement, or an intoxicating substance treatment requirement, the offender is not to be treated as having failed to comply with the order on the ground only that the offender had refused to undergo any surgical, electrical or other treatment, in the opinion of the court, the refusal was reasonable having regard to all the circumstances.

If the court deals with the offender for the offence, it must take into account the extent to which the offender has complied with the order. The order must be revoked.

If the order does not contain an unpaid work requirement, the court may add an unpaid work requirement requiring the offender to perform between 20 and 240 hours work. The court may not impose an extended activity requirement, or a fostering requirement, if the order does not already impose such a requirement.

If the original order imposes a fostering requirement, the court may substitute a new fostering requirement ending not later than 18 months from the date on which the original order was made.

If the offender has wilfully and persistently failed to comply with an order, and the court is dealing with the offender for the original offence, the court may impose a youth rehabilitation order with intensive supervision and surveillance.

If the order is a youth rehabilitation order with intensive supervision and surveillance, and the offence for which it was imposed was punishable with imprisonment, the court may impose a custodial sentence notwithstanding the general restrictions on imposing discretionary custodial sentences.

If the order is a youth rehabilitation order with intensive supervision and surveillance which was imposed following the breach of an earlier order, and the original offence was not punishable with imprisonment, the court may deal with the offender by making a detention and training order for a term not exceeding four months.

Revocation of order

If an application is made by the offender or responsible officer to the appropriate court, and it appears to the court to be in the interests of justice to do so, having regard to circumstances which have arisen since the order was made, the court may either revoke the order, or revoke the order, and deal with the offender, for the offence in respect of which the order was made, in any way in which the court could have dealt with the offender for that offence. The circumstances in which a youth rehabilitation order may be revoked include the offender's making good progress or responding satisfactorily to supervision or treatment. If the court revokes the order and deals with the offender for the original offence, the court must take into account the extent to which the offender has complied with the requirements of the order.

Subsequent conviction

Where an order **is in force** and the offender is convicted of an offence by a youth court or other magistrates' court, and the order was made by a youth court or other magistrates' court, or was made by the Crown Court with a direction that further proceedings should be in the youth court or magistrates court, and the court is dealing with the offender for the further offence, the court may revoke the order and may deal with the offender, for the offence in respect of which the order was made, in any way in which it could have dealt with the offender for that offence.

The court must not revoke the order and deal with the offender for the original offence, unless it considers that it would be in the interests of justice to do so, having regard to circumstances which have arisen since the youth rehabilitation order was made. The sentencing court must take into account the extent to which the offender has complied with the order.

If the youth rehabilitation order was made by the Crown Court, the youth court or magistrates' court may commit the offender in custody, or on bail to the Crown Court.

If an offender appears before the Crown Court while an **order is in force**, having been committed by the magistrates' court to the Crown Court for sentence, or is convicted by the Crown Court of an offence **while an order is in force**, the Crown Court may revoke the order and may deal with the offender, for the offence in respect of which the order was made, *in any way in which the court which made the order could have dealt with the offender for that offence.*

The Crown Court must not deal with the offender for the original offence unless it considers that it would be in the interests of justice to do so, having regard to circumstances which have arisen since the youth rehabilitation order was made. The Crown Court must take into account the extent to which the offender has complied with the order.

If the offender has been committed to the Crown Court to be dealt with in respect of a youth rehabilitation order following a conviction by a youth

court or magistrates' court, the Crown Court may deal with the offender
for the later offence in any way which the youth court or magistrates'
court' could have dealt with the offender for that offence.

Part 2:

Maximum Sentences (Indictable Offences)

This part sets out the maximum sentences available to the Crown Court for the offences which are most commonly tried on indictment or dealt with in the Crown Court.

To use this part, identify the statute and section concerned by reference to the statement of offence in the indictment. Offences are listed by statute and section, with a brief reference to the nature of the offence. Where the same section creates different offences, the maximum sentence for each offence is set out separately.

LIBRARY, UNIVERSITY OF CHESTER

Part 3

Maximum Sentences (Indictable Offences)

This part sets out the maximum sentences available to the Crown Court for the offences which are most commonly dealt with in cases that are dealt with by the Crown Court.

The sentences given in the Standard sentence columns and by reference to the relevant parts of the Sentencing Guidelines. Offences are listed by reference to an offence with a brief reference to the nature of the offence. Where appropriate cross-references are given but further information is also provided is set out separately.

Aviation Security Act 1982

Section 1 (hijacking)	**Life**
Section 2 (destroying aircraft)	**Life**
Section 3 (endangering safety of aircraft)	**Life**
Section 4 (possessing dangerous article)	**5 years**
Section 6 (inducing offence)	**Life**

Note:

Sections 1, 2, 3 and 4:

Specified offence (Criminal Justice Act 2003 Sch.15)

Scheduled offence (Sexual Offences Act 2003 Sch.5)

Sections 1, 2, 3 and 6:

Powers of Criminal Courts (Sentencing) Act 2000 s.91 applies.

Bail Act 1976

Section 6 (failing to surrender)	**12 months**

Note: Where an offender is dealt with by the Crown Court for a bail offence, otherwise than on a committal by a magistrates' court under Bail Act 1976 s.6(6), he is to be dealt with as if the bail offence were a contempt of court. An offender under the age of 18 may not be committed to custody for a bail offence.

Bribery Act 2010

Section 1 (bribery of another person)	**10 years**
Section 2 (requesting, agreeing to accept or accepting a bribe)	**10 years**
Section 6 (bribery of foreign public official)	**10 years**
Section 7 (failure of commercial organization to prevent bribery)	**Fine**

Child Abduction Act 1984

Section 1 (taking out of United Kingdom without consent)	**7 years**
Section 2 (taking child out of lawful control)	**7 years**

Penalty provision: section 4.

Note:

Sections 1 and 2: Scheduled offence for purposes of Sexual Offences Act 2003 Sch.5.

Offences against this Act are not specified offences for the purposes of the Criminal Justice Act 2003 Sch.15.

Children and Young Persons Act 1933

Section 1 (ill-treatment or neglect etc.)	**10 years**
Section 26 (procuring child to go abroad by false representation)	**2 years**

Note:

Section 1:

Specified offence (Criminal Justice Act 2003 Sch.15).

Scheduled offence (Sexual Offences Act 2003 Sch.5).

Companies Act 2006

Section 993 (fraudulent trading)	**10 years**
(if offence committed on or after January 15, 2007).	

Computer Misuse Act 1990

Section 1 (securing unauthorised access)	**2 years***
Section 2 (unauthorised access with intent)	**5 years**
Section 3 (unauthorised modification)	**10 years****

*(if offence committed on or after October 1, 2008)
**(if offence committed on or after October 1, 2008; otherwise 5 years)

Contempt of Court Act 1981

Section 14 (contempt of superior court)	**2 years**

Note: A committal for contempt is not a sentence of imprisonment or detention in a young offender institution for the purposes of Criminal Justice Act 1991 s.51(2). An offender under the age of 18 may not be committed to custody for contempt.

Copyright Designs and Patents Act 1988

Offences under s.107(1)(a), (b), (d)(iv) or (e)	**10 years**
Offences under s.107(2A)	**2 years**

Crime and Disorder Act 1998

Section 29(1)(a) (racially or religiously aggravated unlawful wounding)	**7 years**
Section 29(1)(b) (racially or religiously aggravated assault occasioning actual bodily harm)	**7 years**
Section 29(1)(c) (racially or religiously aggravated common assault)	**2 years**
Section 30 (racially or religiously aggravated criminal damage)	**14 years**
Section 31(1)(a) (racially or religiously aggravated causing fear of violence)	**2 years**
Section 31(1)(b) (racially or religiously aggravated intentional harassment)	**2 years**
Section 32(1)(a) (racially or religiously aggravated harassment)	**2 years**
Section 32(1)(b) (racially or religiously aggravated causing fear of violence)	**7 years**

Note:

Offence under s.29:

Specified offence (Criminal Justice Act 2003 Sch.15).

Scheduled offence (Sexual Offences Act 2003 Sch.5).

Offence under s.31(1)(a) or (b):

Specified offence (Criminal Justice Act 2003 Sch.15).

Criminal Attempts Act 1981

Section 1 (attempted murder)	**Life**
Section 1 (attempting indictable offence)	**As for offence in question**

Note: Special provisions apply to attempted incest. See under Sexual Offences Act 1956.

Note: An attempt to commit an offence which is a specified offence (Criminal Justice Act 2003 Sch.15), or a scheduled offence (Sexual Offences Act 2003 Schs 2 or 5) is also a specified offence, an offence against a child or a scheduled offence. An attempt to commit an offence which is a "serious offence" for the purposes of the P.C.C.(S.)A. 2000 s.109, is not itself a "serious offence" unless it is listed as such in s.109.

Criminal Damage Act 1971

Section 1(1) (criminal damage)	**10 years**

Note: if the value of the damage does not exceed £5,000 and the matter comes before the Crown Court under Criminal Justice Act 1988 ss.40 or 41, or P.C.C.(S.)A. 2000 s.6, the maximum sentence is three months.

Section 1(2) (criminal damage with intent to endanger life)	**Life**
Section 1(3) (arson)	**Life**
Section 2 (threatening to damage property)	**10 years**
Section 3 (possession with intent)	**10 years**

Penalty provision: section 4.

Note: Arson and criminal damage endangering life (s.1(2)).

Specified offence (Criminal Justice Act 2003 Sch.15).

Scheduled offence (Sexual Offences Act 2003 Sch.5).

P.C.C.(S.)A. 2000 s.91 applies.

Criminal Justice Act 1925

Section 36(1) (making false statement to procure passport) **2 years**

Criminal Justice Act 1961

Section 22 (harbouring escaped prisoner) **10 years**

Criminal Justice Act 1988

Section 134 (torture) **Life**

Note:

Section 134:

Specified offence (Criminal Justice Act 2003 Sch.15).

Scheduled offence (Sexual Offences Act 2003 Schs 2, 5).

P.C.C.(S.)A. 2000 s.91 applies.

Section 139 (possessing sharp bladed or pointed instrument) **4 years**
(*if offence was committed before February 12, 2007; two years*)
Section 139A (possessing offensive weapon on school premises) **4 years**
Section 139AA (threatening with article with a blade or point or offensive weapon) **4 years**
Section 160 (possessing indecent photograph of child) **5 years**
(If the offence was committed on or after January 11, 2001; otherwise six months).

Note:

Section 160:

Specified offence (Criminal Justice Act 2003 Sch.15).

Scheduled offence (Sexual Offences Act 2003 Sch.3), if the indecent photographs, etc. showed persons under 16 and (if the offence was committed after May 1, 2004) the offender was over 18 or sentenced to a term of imprisonment of at least 12 months (see s.131).

Criminal Justice Act 1993

Section 61 (insider dealing)   **7 years**

Criminal Justice (International Co-operation) Act 1990

Section 12 (manufacturing or supplying scheduled substance)	**14 years**
Section 19 (having possession of a Class A controlled drug on a ship)	**Life**
Section 19 (having possession of a Class B controlled drug on a ship)	**14 years**
Section 19 (having possession of a Class C controlled drug on a ship)	**14 years**

Note: Offences under ss.12 and 19 are drug trafficking offences for the purposes of the Drug Trafficking Act 1994 and the Proceeds of Crime Act 2002 Sch.2.

Criminal Justice and Public Order Act 1994

Section 51 (intimidating witness)   **5 years**

Criminal Law Act 1967

Section 4 (assisting offender)

Sentence for principal offence fixed by law	**10 years**
Maximum sentence for principal offence 14 years	**7 years**
Maximum sentence for principal offence 10 years	**5 years**
Otherwise (normally five years)	**3 years**

Criminal Law Act 1977

Section 1 (conspiracy to commit offence punishable by life imprisonment)	**Life**
Section 1 (conspiracy to commit offence for which no maximum is provided)	**Life**
Section 1 (conspiracy to commit offence with specified maximum term)	**Maximum term for offence in question**
Section 51 (bomb hoax)	**7 years**

Customs and Excise Management Act 1979

Section 50 (importing undutied or prohibited goods)	**7 years**
Section 68 (evading prohibition of exportation)	**7 years**
Section 170 (evading duty, or prohibition)	**7 years**

Note: Where an offence under ss.50, 68 or 170 relates to Class A drugs, the maximum is life imprisonment; where the offence relates to Class B or Class C drugs, the maximum is 14 years.

Where an offence under ss.50, 68 or 170 relates to goods prohibited by the Forgery and Counterfeiting Act 1981 ss.20 or 21, the maximum sentence is 10 years.

Where an offence under ss.50, 68 or 170 relates to certain prohibited weapons within the meaning of the Firearms Act 1968 s.5(1) (excluding weapons falling within ss.5(1)(b) or 5(1A)(b) to (g)), the maximum is 10 years.

Section 170B (taking preparatory steps)	**7 years**

Offences involving the importation or exportation of controlled drugs are drug trafficking offences for the purposes of the Drug Trafficking Act 1994 and the Proceeds of Crime Act 2002 Sch.2.

Offences involving the importation or exportation of controlled drugs: P.C.C.(S.)A. 2000 s.91 applies.

Offences involving importation of indecent materials:

Specified offence (Criminal Justice Act 2003 Sch.15)

Scheduled offence (Sexual Offences Act 2003 Sch.3, if the indecent photographs etc. showed persons under 16 and (if the offence was committed after May 1, 2004) the offender was over 18 or sentenced to a term of imprisonment of at least 12 months (see s.131).

Domestic Violence, Crime and Victims Act 2004

Section 5 (causing or allowing death of child)   **14 years**
Section 5 (causing or allowing serious injury)   **10 years**

Specified offences (Criminal Justice Act 2003 Sch.15).

Explosive Substances Act 1883

Section 2 (causing explosion likely to endanger life)   **Life**
Section 3 (attempting to cause explosion, or possessing
  explosive substance with intent)   **Life**
Section 4 (making or possessing explosive substance)   **14 years**

Note:

Sections 2 and 3:

Specified offence (Criminal Justice Act 2003 Sch.15).

Scheduled offence (Sexual Offences Act 2003 Schs 2, 5).

Sections 2, 3 and 4:

P.C.C.(S.)A. 2000 s.91 applies.

Firearms Act 1968

Section 1 (possessing firearm without certificate)   **5 years**
Section 1 (possessing shortened shotgun)   **7 years**
Section 2 (possessing shotgun without certificate)   **5 years**
Section 3 (selling firearm, etc.)   **5 years**

Section 4 (shortening shotgun)	**7 years**
Section 5 (possessing, etc., prohibited weapon)	**10 years**
Section 16 (possessing firearm with intent to endanger life)	**Life**
Section 16A (possessing firearm with intent to cause fear of violence)	**10 years**
Section 17 (using firearm to prevent arrest, or while committing scheduled offence)	**Life**
Section 18 (carrying firearm with intent to commit offence)	**Life**
Section 19 (carrying firearm other than an airweapon in public place)	**7 years**

Note: If the firearm is an imitation firearm, the maximum sentence for an offence committed **before October 1, 2007** is six months; after that date, 12 months.

Section 20 (trespassing with firearm)	**5 years**
Section 21 (possessing firearm as former prisoner, etc.)	**5 years**

Penalty provision: Schedule 6, as amended by Criminal Justice and Public Order Act 1994 Sch.8.

Note:

Sections 16, 16A, 17(1) and (2), 18:

Specified offence (Criminal Justice Act 2003 Sch.15).

Scheduled offence (Sexual Offences Act 2003 Schs 2, 5).

Serious offence (P.C.C.(S.)A. 2000 s.109).

P.C.C.(S.)A. 2000 s.91 applies.

Section 5 (with exceptions).

Required minimum sentence applies (Firearms Act 1968 s.51A).

Sections 16, 16A, 17, 18, 19, 20(1).

Required minimum sentence applies if firearm is a prohibited weapon.

Forgery and Counterfeiting Act 1981

Section 1 (making false instrument with intent)	**10 years**
Section 2 (making copy of false instrument with intent)	**10 years**
Section 3 (using false instrument with intent)	**10 years**
Section 4 (using copy of false instrument)	**10 years**
Section 5(1) (custody or control of false instrument with intent)	**10 years**
Section 5(2) (custody or control of false instrument, no intent)	**2 years**
Section 5(3) (making machine, etc., with intent)	**10 years**
Section 5(4) (making machine, etc., no intent)	**2 years**

Penalty provision:

Section 6.

Fraud Act 2006

Section 1 (fraud)	**10 years**
Section 6 (possession of article for use in fraud)	**5 years**
Section 7 (making or supplying article for use in fraud)	**10 years**

Identity Documents Act 2010

Section 4 (possession of false identity document with improper intent)	**10 years**
Section 5 (possession of apparatus etc. with improper intent)	**10 years**
Section 6 (possession of false identity document)	**2 years**

Immigration Act 1971

Section 24A (obtaining admission by deception)	**2 years**
Section 25 (facilitating illegal entry)	**14 years**
Section 25A (assisting asylum seeker)	**14 years**
Section 25B (assisting entry in breach of deportation order)	**14 years**

Incitement to Disaffection Act 1934

Section 1 (seducing member of forces from duty)   **2 years**
Section 2 (possessing document, etc.)   **2 years**

Penalty provision: section 3.

Indecency with Children Act 1960

Section 1 (gross indecency with child)   **10 years**
(If the offence was committed on or after October 1, 1997; otherwise two years).

Note: This Act was repealed by the Sexual Offences Act 2003 with effect from May 1, 2004, but it is thought that its practical effect has been preserved by the Interpretation Act 1978 s.16, See note to Sexual Offences Act 1956.

Specified offence (Criminal Justice Act 2003 Sch.15).

Scheduled offence (Sexual Offences Act 2003 Sch.2).

P.C.C.(S.)A. 2000 s.91 does not apply.

Indecent Displays (Control) Act 1981

Section 1 (displaying indecent matter)   **2 years**

Penalty provision: section 4.

Infanticide Act 1938

Section 1 (infanticide)   **Life**

Note:

Specified offence (Criminal Justice Act 2003 Sch.15).

Scheduled offence (Sexual Offences Act 2003 Schs 2, 5).

P.C.C.(S.)A. 2000 s.91 applies.

Infant Life (Preservation) Act 1929

Section 1 (child destruction) **Life**

Note:

Specified offence (Criminal Justice Act 2003 Sch.15).

Scheduled offence (Sexual Offences Act 2003 Sch.5).

P.C.C.(S.)A. 2000 s.91 applies.

Knives Act 1997

Section 1 (marketing combat knife)	**2 years**
Section 2 (publishing material)	**2 years**

Mental Health Act 1983

Section 126 (possession of false document)	**2 years**
Section 127 (ill-treating patient)	**5 years**
(if the offence was committed on or after October 1, 2007; otherwise two years)	
Section 128 (assisting absconded patient)	**2 years**

Merchant Shipping Act 1995

Section 58 (endangering ship)	**2 years**

Misuse of Drugs Act 1971

Section 4(2) (producing Class A drug)	**Life**
Section 4(2) (producing Class B drug)	**14 years**

Section 4(2) (producing Class C drug)	**14 years**
Section 4(3) (supplying Class A drug)	**Life**
Section 4(3) (supplying Class B drug)	**14 years**
Section 4(3) (supplying Class C drug)	**14 years**
Section 5(2) (possessing Class A drug)	**7 years**
Section 5(2) (possessing Class B drug)	**5 years**
Section 5(2) (possessing Class C drug)	**2 years**
Section 5(3) (possessing Class A drug with intent to supply)	**Life**
Section 5(3) (possessing Class B drug with intent to supply)	**14 years**
Section 5(3) (possessing Class C drug with intent to supply)	**14 years**
Section 6(2) (cultivating cannabis plant)	**14 years**
Section 8 (occupier of premises permitting supply, etc. of Class A drugs)	**14 years**
Section 8 (occupier of premises permitting supply, etc. of Class B drugs)	**14 years**
Section 8 (occupier of premises permitting supply, etc. of Class C drugs)	**14 years**
Section 9 (opium)	**14 years**
Section 11(2) (contravention of directions)	**2 years**
Section 12(6) (contravention of prohibition on prescribing in relation to Class A drug)	**14 years**
Section 12(6) (contravention of prohibition on prescribing in relation to Class B drug)	**14 years**
Section 12(6) (contravention of prohibition on prescribing in relation to Class C drug)	**14 years**
Section 13(3) (contravention of prohibition on supplying in relation to Class A drug)	**14 years**
Section 13(3) (contravention of prohibition on supplying in relation to Class B drug)	**14 years**
Section 13(3) (contravention of prohibition on supplying in relation to Class C drug)	**14 years**
Section 17(4) (giving false information)	**2 years**
Section 18 (contravention of regulations, etc.)	**2 years**
Section 20 (assisting offence outside United Kingdom)	**14 years**
Section 23 (obstructing search)	**2 years**

Penalty provision: Schedule 4.

Note: Offences under ss.4(2) or (3), 5(3), 20, 49, 50 and 51 are drug trafficking offences for the purposes of the Drug Trafficking Act 1994. Offences under ss.(2) or (3), 5(3), and 8 are drug trafficking offences for the purposes of the Proceeds of Crime Act 2002 Sch.2.

Section 4(3):

Obscene Publications Act 1959

Section 2 (publishing obscene article or having article for
  publication)   **5 years**

(if the offence was committed on or after January 26, 2009, otherwise 3
years)

Offences against the Person Act 1861

Section 4 (soliciting to murder)	**Life**
Section 16 (threatening to kill)	**10 years**
Section 18 (wounding with intent to cause grievous bodily harm)	**Life**
Section 20 (unlawful wounding)	**5 years**
Section 21 (choking, etc., with intent)	**Life**
Section 22 (administering drug with intent)	**Life**
Section 23 (administering noxious thing to endanger life)	**10 years**
Section 24 (administering noxious thing to injure, aggrieve or annoy)	**5 years**
Section 27 (abandoning child)	**5 years**
Section 28 (causing grievous bodily harm by explosion)	**Life**
Section 29 (using explosives with intent, throwing corrosive substance with intent)	**Life**
Section 30 (placing explosive substance with intent)	**14 years**
Section 31 (setting spring gun, etc.)	**5 years**
Section 32 (endangering safety of railway passengers)	**Life**
Section 33 (throwing object with intent to endanger rail passenger)	**Life**
Section 34 (endangering rail passenger by neglect)	**2 years**
Section 35 (causing grievous bodily harm by wanton driving)	**2 years**
Section 36 (obstructing minister of religion)	**2 years**
Section 38 (assault with intent to resist arrest)	**2 years**
Section 47 (assault occasioning actual bodily harm)	**5 years**
Section 58 (procuring miscarriage)	**Life**
Section 59 (supplying instrument, etc.)	**5 years**
Section 60 (concealment of birth)	**2 years**

Note: Offences under the following sections are specified offences for the
purposes of the Criminal Justice Act 2003 Sch.15: ss.4, 16, 18, 20, 21, 22,
23, 27, 28, 29, 30, 31, 32, 35, 37, 38, 47.

Offences under the following sections are scheduled offences for the
purposes of the Sexual Offences Act 2003 Sch.5: ss.4, 16, 18, 20, 21, 22, 23,
27, 28, 29, 30, 31, 32, 35, 37, 38, 47.

Official Secrets Act 1911

Section 1 (act prejudicial to safety of state) **14 years**
Penalty provision: Official Secrets Act 1920 s.8(1)

Official Secrets Act 1920

Section 1(1) (gaining admission to prohibited place) **2 years**
Section 1(2) (retaining document, etc.) **2 years**
Section 3 (interfering with police officer or sentry) **2 years**

Penalty provision: section 8(2).

Official Secrets Act 1989

Section 1 (disclosing information) **2 years**
Section 3 (Crown servant making disclosure) **2 years**
Section 4 (unauthorised disclosure) **2 years**
Section 5 (unauthorised disclosure by recipient) **2 years**
Section 6 (unauthorised disclosure) **2 years**

Penalty provision: section 10.

Perjury Act 1911

Section 1 (witness making untrue statement) **7 years**
Section 1A (false statement for foreign proceedings) **2 years**

Prevention of Crime Act 1953

Section 1 (possessing offensive weapon) **4 years**
Section 1A (threatening with offensive weapon in public) **4 years**

Note: There is a required sentence for those aged 16+ at conviction.

Prison Act 1952

Section 39 (assisting escape)	**10 years**
Bringing etc list A article into prison (Prison Act 1952 s.40B)	**10 years**
Bringing etc list B article into prison (Prison Act 1952 s.40C)	**2 years**
Bringing etc list C article into prison (Prison Act 1952 s.40C)	**(Summary) fine level 3**
Transmitting document etc (Prison Act 1952 s.40D)	**2 years**

Prison Security Act 1992

Section 1 (prison mutiny)	**10 years**

Proceeds of Crime Act 2002

Section 327	**14 years**
Section 328	**14 years**
Section 329	**14 years**
Section 330	**5 years**
Section 331	**5 years**
Section 332	**5 years**

Protection from Eviction Act 1977

Section 1 (depriving residential occupier of occupation)	**2 years**

Protection from Harassment Act 1997

Section 3 (breach of injunction)	**5 years**
Section 4 (causing fear of violence)	**5 years**
Section 4A (stalking involving fear of violence or serious alarm or distress)	**5 years**

Protection of Children Act 1978

Section 1 (taking, distributing, possessing, publishing
indecent photograph of child) . **10 years**

(If the offence was committed on or after January 11, 2001; otherwise three years).

Penalty provision: section 6.

Note:

Section 1:

Specified offence (Criminal Justice Act 2003 Sch.15).

Scheduled offence (Sexual Offences Act 2003 Sch.3, if the indecent photographs etc. showed persons under 16 and (if the offence was committed after May 1, 2004), the offender was over 18 or sentenced to a term of imprisonment of at least twelve months (see s.131).

Public Order Act 1936

Section 2 (unlawful organisation) **2 years**

Penalty provision: section 7.

Public Order Act 1986

Section 1 (riot) **10 years**
Section 2 (violent disorder) **5 years**
Section 3 (affray) **3 years**
Section 18 (using words to stir up racial hatred) **7 years**
Section 19 (distributing material to stir up racial hatred) **7 years**
Section 20 (performing play to stir up racial hatred) **7 years**
Section 21 (distributing recording to stir up racial
hatred) **7 years**
Section 22 (broadcasting programme) **7 years**
Section 23 (possessing material to stir up racial hatred) **7 years**

Penalty provision: section 27(3).

Section 38 (contaminating goods)   **10 years**

Note: offences against the following provisions are specified offences for the purposes of the Criminal Justice Act 2003 Sch.15: ss.1 (riot), 2 (violent disorder), 3 (affray).

Representation of the People Act 1983

Section 60 (personation)   **2 years**

Road Traffic Act 1988

Section 1 (causing death by dangerous driving)   **14 years**
Section 1A (causing serious injury by dangerous driving)   **5 years**
Section 2 (dangerous driving)   **2 years**

Section 2B (causing death by careless or inconsiderate driving)   **5 years**
Section 3A (causing death by careless driving, having consumed alcohol)   **14 years**
Section 3ZB (causing death by driving while unlicenced, disqualified or uninsured)   **2 years**
Section 4(1) (driving while unfit)   **6 months**
Section 5(1) (driving with excess alcohol)   **6 months**

Penalty provision: Road Traffic Offenders Act 1988 Sch. 2.

Note:

Sections 1, 3A:

Specified offence (Criminal Justice Act 2003 Sch.15).

Scheduled offence (Sexual Offences Act 2003 Sch.5).

Serious Crime Act 2007

Section 44 (encouraging or assisting commission of offence) . . . if the anticipated offence is murder, life imprisonment, otherwise the maximum sentence for the anticipated or reference offence.

Section 45 (encouraging or assisting commission of
offence, believing it will be committed) . . . if the anticipated offence is murder, life imprisonment, otherwise the
maximum sentence for the anticipated or reference
offence.
Section 46 (encouraging or assisting commission of one
or more offences) . . . if the anticipated or reference
offence is murder, life imprisonment, otherwise the maximum sentence for the anticipated or reference offence.

If the offence whose commission is encouraged or assisted is a specified
offence for the purposes of the Criminal Justice Act 2003 Sch.15, an
offence under ss 44, 45 or 46 is also a specified offence for that purpose.

Sexual Offences Act 1956

Most sections of the Sexual Offences Act 1956 are repealed with effect
from May 1, 2004, by the Sexual Offences Act 2003. References in other
statutes (such as the P.C.C.(S.)A. 2000 s.161) are also for the most part
repealed by the Sexual Offences Act 2003. The liability of an offender to be
sentenced for a sexual offence committed before May 1, 2004, depends on
the Interpretation Act 1978 s.16, which provides:

> "Without prejudice to section 15, where an Act repeals an enactment,
> the repeal does not, unless the contrary intention appears,—
> (c) affect any right, privilege, obligation or liability acquired,
>   accrued or incurred under that enactment;
> (d) affect any penalty, forfeiture or punishment incurred in respect
>   of any offence committed against that enactment;
> (e) affect any investigation, legal proceeding or remedy in respect
>   of any such right, privilege, obligation, liability, penalty, forfei-
>   ture or punishment; and any such investigation, legal proceed-
>   ing or remedy may be instituted, continued or enforced, and
>   any such penalty, forfeiture or punishment may be imposed, as
>   if the repealing Act had not been passed."

It appears that this section preserves the effect of the Sexual Offences
Act 1956, and preserves the effect of statutory provisions referring to
provisions of that Act, in respect of offences committed on or before May 1,
2004.

Section 1 (rape)	**Life**
Section 2 (procurement of woman by threats)	**2 years**
Section 3 (procurement by false pretences)	**2 years**

Section 4 (administering drugs)	**2 years**
Section 5 (intercourse with girl under 13)	**Life**
Section 6 (unlawful sexual intercourse with girl under 16)	**2 years**
Section 7 (intercourse with defective)	**2 years**
Section 9 (procurement of defective)	**2 years**
Section 10 (incest by man with girl under 13)	**Life**
(attempt, seven years)	
Section 10 (incest by man)	**7 years**
(attempt, two years)	
Section 11 (incest by woman)	**7 years**
(attempt, two years)	
Section 12 (buggery with person under 16)	**Life**
Section 12 (buggery with animal)	**Life**
Section 12 (buggery of person under 18 by person over 21)	**5 years**
Section 12 (other forms of buggery)	**2 years**
Section 13 (indecency by man over 21 with man under 18)	**5 years**
Section 13 (indecency by males)	**2 years**
Section 14 (indecent assault on woman)	**10 years**

(If the offence was committed on or after September 16, 1985: otherwise two years, unless the victim was under 13 and her age was stated in the indictment, in which case the maximum is five years).

Section 15 (indecent assault on male)	**10 years**
Section 16 (assault with intent to bugger)	**10 years**
Section 17 (abduction)	**14 years**
Section 19 (abduction of girl under 18)	**2 years**
Section 20 (abduction of girl under 16)	**2 years**
Section 21 (abduction of defective)	**2 years**
Section 22 (causing prostitution)	**2 years**
Section 23 (procuring girl under 21)	**2 years**
Section 24 (detention in brothel)	**2 years**
Section 25 (permitting premises to be used by girl under 13)	**Life**
Section 26 (permitting premises to be used)	**2 years**
Section 27 (permitting defective to use premises)	**2 years**
Section 28 (causing prostitution of girl under 16)	**2 years**
Section 29 (causing prostitution of defective)	**2 years**
Section 30 (living on earnings of prostitution)	**7 years**
Section 31 (controlling prostitute)	**7 years**
Section 32 (man soliciting)	**2 years**
Section 33A (keeping brothel used for prostitution)	**7 years**

Offences under the following sections are specified offences for the purposes of the Criminal Justice Act 2003 Sch.15: ss.1, 2, 3, 4, 5, 6, 7, 9, 10,

11, 14, 15, 16, 17, 19, 20, 21, 22, 23, 24, 25, 26, 27, 28, 29, 32, 33. (offences contrary to s.13 are not specified offences).

Offences under the following provisions are sexual offences for the purposes of the Sexual Offences Act 2003 Sch.3, if the required conditions are satisfied: ss.1, 5, 6 (if offender 20 or over), 12 (if other party under 18), 12 (if offender over 20 and other party under 18), 14 (if victim under 18, or offender sentenced to 30 months or more or to a hospital order), 15 (if victim under 18, or offender sentenced to 30 months or more or to a hospital order), 16 (if victim under 18), 28 (if girl under 16).

All offences under the Sexual Offences Act 1956, except for offences under sections 30, 31, 33, 34, 35 and 36 were "sexual offences" for the purposes of the P.C.C.(S.)A. 2000 s.161.

P.C.C.(S.)A. 2000 s.91 applies to all offences punishable with imprisonment for 14 years or more, and to offences under ss.14 and 15.

Sexual Offences Act 2003

Section 1 (rape)	**Life**
Section 2 (assault by penetration)	**Life**
Section 3 (sexual assault)	**10 years**
Section 4 (causing sexual activity with penetration)	**Life**
Section 4 (causing sexual activity without penetration)	**10 years**
Section 5 (penetration of child under 13)	**Life**
Section 6 (assault of person under 13 by penetration)	**Life**
Section 7 (sexual assault on person under 13)	**14 years**
Section 8 (causing person under 13 to engage in sexual activity involving penetration)	**Life**
Section 8 (causing person under 13 to engage in sexual activity without penetration)	**14 years**
Section 9 (sexual activity with person under 16)	**14 years**
Section 10 (causing person under 16 to engage in sexual activity)	**14 years**
Section 11 (sexual activity in presence of person under 16)	**10 years**
Section 12 (causing person under 16 to watch sexual act)	**10 years**
Section 13 (child sex offence committed by person under 18)	**5 years**
Section 14 (arranging child sex offence)	**14 years**
Section 15 (meeting person under 16 with intent following grooming)	**10 years**
Section 16 (abuse of trust by sexual activity)	**5 years**

Section 17 (abuse of trust by causing sexual activity)	**5 years**
Section 18 (abuse of trust by sexual activity in presence of child)	**5 years**
Section 19 (abuse of trust by causing child to watch sexual act)	**5 years**
Section 25 (sexual activity by person over 18 with family member under 18)	**14 years**
Section 25 (sexual activity by person under 18 with family member under 18)	**5 years**
Section 26 (person over 18 inciting family member under 18 to engage in sexual activity)	**14 years**
Section 26 (person under 18 inciting family member under 18 to engage in sexual activity)	**5 years**
Section 30 (sexual activity involving penetration with person with mental disorder)	**Life**
Section 30 (sexual activity not involving penetration with person with mental disorder)	**14 years**
Section 31 (causing or inciting sexual activity involving penetration by person with mental disorder)	**Life**
Section 31 (causing or inciting sexual activity not involving penetration by person with mental disorder)	**14 years**
Section 32 (engaging in sexual activity in presence of person with mental disorder)	**10 years**
Section 33 (causing person with mental disorder to watch sexual act)	**10 years**
Section 34 (offering inducement to person with mental disorder to engage in sexual act involving penetration)	**Life**
Section 34 (offering inducement to person with mental disorder to engage in sexual act not involving penetration)	**14 years**
Section 35 (inducing person with mental disorder to engage in sexual act involving penetration)	**Life**
Section 35 (inducing person with mental disorder to engage in sexual act not involving penetration)	**14 years**
Section 36 (causing person with mental disorder to watch sexual act by inducement etc.)	**10 years**
Section 37 (causing person with mental disorder to watch third party sexual act by inducement etc.)	**10 years**
Section 38 (sexual acts involving penetration by care worker with person with mental disorder)	**14 years**
Section 38 (sexual acts not involving penetration by care worker with person with mental disorder)	**10 years**
Section 39 (care worker inciting person with mental disorder engage in sexual act involving penetration)	**14 years**
Section 39 (care worker inciting person with mental disorder engage in sexual act not involving penetration)	**10 years**

Section 40 (care worker engaging in sexual act in presence of person with mental disorder)	**7 years**
Section 41 (care worker causing person with mental disorder to watch sexual act)	**7 years**
Section 47 (paying for sexual service involving penetration by person under 13)	**Life**
Section 47 (paying for sexual service by person under 16)	**14 years**
Section 47 (paying for sexual service by person under 18)	**7 years**
Section 48 (causing person under 18 to become involved in prostitution or pornography)	**14 years**
Section 49 (controlling prostitution by person under 18)	**14 years**
Section 50 (facilitating prostitution by person under 18)	**14 years**
Section 52 (causing or inciting prostitution)	**7 years**
Section 53 (controlling prostitution for gain)	**7 years**
Section 57 (arranging arrival for purposes of prostitution)	**14 years**
Section 58 (facilitating travel for purposes of prostitution)	**14 years**
Section 59 (facilitating departure for purposes of prostitution)	**14 years**
Section 59A (trafficking people for sexual exploitation)—substituted for ss.57–59 above from April 6, 2013	**14 years**
Section 61 (administering substance with intent to enable sexual activity)	**10 years**
Section 62 (committing offence with intent to commit sexual offence)	**10 years**
Section 63 (trespass with intent to commit sexual offence)	**10 years**
Section 64 (sexual penetration of adult relative)	**2 years**
Section 65 (consenting to sexual penetration by adult relative)	**2 years**
Section 66 (intentional exposure)	**2 years**
Section 67 (observing private act)	**2 years**
Section 69 (sexual act with animal)	**2 years**
Section 70 (sexual penetration of corpse)	**2 years**

Note: Offences under the following provisions are specified offences for the purposes of the Criminal Justice Act 2003 Sch.15: ss.1, 2, 3, 4, 5, 6, 7, 8, 9, 10, 11, 12, 13, 14, 15, 16, 17, 18, 19, 25, 26, 30, 31, 32, 33, 34, 35, 36, 37, 38, 39, 40, 41, 47, 48, 49, 50, 52, 53, 57, 58, 59, 61, 62, 63, 64, 65, 66, 67, 69, 70.

Offences against the following provisions are scheduled sexual offences for the purposes of the Sexual Offences Act 2003 Sch.3, if the required conditions are satisfied: ss.1, 2, 3*, 4, 5, 6, 7*, 8, 9, 10, 11, 12, 13*, 14*, 15, 16, 17, 18, 19*, 25*, 26*, 30, 31, 32, 33, 34, 35, 36, 37, 38*, 39*, 40*, 41*, 47*, 48*, 49*, 50*, 51, 52, 53, 57, 58, 59, 61, 62*, 63*, 64*, 65*, 66*, 67*, 69*, 70*.

Conditions apply to provisions marked with asterisk. See Current Sentencing Practice H11–1G.

Offences against the following provisions are sexual offences for the purposes of the P.C.C.(S.)A. 2000 s.161: any provision of Pt 1 of the Act except ss.52, 53, or 71.

Sexual Offences (Amendment) Act 2000

This Act is repealed by the Sexual Offences Act 2003; but see the note to the Sexual Offences Act 1956.

Section 3 (abuse of position of trust)	**5 years**

Scheduled offence (Sexual Offences Act 2003 Sch.3) if offender 20 or over.

Suicide Act 1961

Section 2 (aiding suicide)	**14 years**

Theatres Act 1968

Section 2 (giving obscene performance)	**3 years**

Theft Act 1968

Section 7 (theft)	**7 years**
Section 8 (robbery)	**Life**
Section 9 (burglary of dwelling)	**14 years**
Section 9 (burglary of building other than dwelling)	**10 years**
Section 10 (aggravated burglary)	**Life**
Section 11 (removing object from public place)	**5 years**
Section 12A (aggravated vehicle taking resulting in death)	**14 years**
Section 12A (aggravated vehicle taking not resulting in death)	**2 years**

Note: if the offence is aggravated vehicle taking by reason of causing damage, and the value of the damage does not exceed £5,000, the offence will normally be dealt with as a summary offence and the maximum sentence is six months.

Section 13 (abstracting electricity)	**5 years**

Section 15 (obtaining by deception)	**10 years**
Section 15A (obtaining money transfer by deception)	**10 years**
Section 16 (obtaining pecuniary advantage)	**5 years**
Section 17 (false accounting)	**7 years**
Section 20 (destroying valuable security etc.)	**7 years**
Section 22 (handling)	**14 years**

Note: offences against the following provisions are specified offences for the purposes of the Criminal Justice Act 2003 Sch.15): 8, 9 (burglary with intent to cause grievous bodily harm, cause criminal damage, or rape: not burglary with intent to steal) ss.9, 12A (aggravated vehicle taking involving death).

Offences under the following provisions are scheduled offences for the purposes of the Sexual Offences Act 2003 Sch.5: s.1 (theft) ss.8, 9, (burglary with intent to cause grievous bodily harm, cause criminal damage or steal), ss.10, 12A (aggravated vehicle taking involving death).

The definition of burglary is amended by the Sexual Offences Act 2003 to omit references to an intent to rape; offences which would formerly have been charged as burglary with intent to rape will now be charged as trespass with intent, contrary to s.63.

Theft Act 1978

Section 1 (obtaining services)	**5 years**
Section 2 (evading liability, etc.)	**5 years**
Section 3 (making off without payment)	**2 years**

Penalty provision: section 4.

Value Added Tax Act 1994

Section 72 (fraudulently evading VAT, etc.)	**7 years**

Violent Crime Reduction Act 2006

Section 28 (using another to hide weapon etc.)

If weapon is weapon to which Criminal Justice Act 1988
    s.141 or 141A applies **4 years**
If weapon is prohibited weapon (with exceptions) and
    offender is over 16 **10 years**
Other cases **5 years**

Part 3

Charts and Tables

Dangerous Offenders—Adults

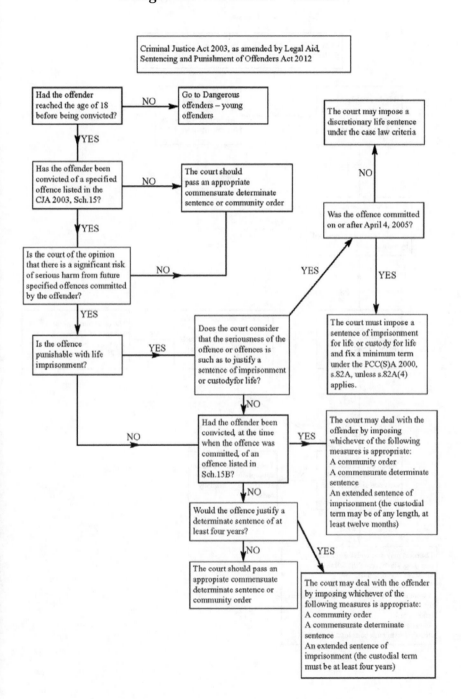

Criminal Justice Act 2003, as amended by Legal Aid, Sentencing and Punishment of Offenders Act 2012

Had the offender reached the age of 18 before being convicted? — NO → Go to Dangerous offenders – young offenders

↓ YES

Has the offender been convicted of a specified offence listed in the CJA 2003, Sch.15? — NO → The court should pass an appropriate commensurate determinate sentence or community order

↓ YES

Is the court of the opinion that there is a significant risk of serious harm from future specified offences committed by the offender? — NO →

↓ YES

Is the offence punishable with life imprisonment? — YES → **Does the court consider that the seriousness of the offence or offences is such as to justify a sentence of imprisonment or custody for life?**

The court may impose a discretionary life sentence under the case law criteria

NO ↑

Was the offence committed on or after April 4, 2005? — YES →

↓ YES

The court must impose a sentence of imprisonment for life or custody for life and fix a minimum term under the PCC(S)A 2000, s.82A, unless s.82A(4) applies.

↓ NO

Had the offender been convicted, at the time when the offence was committed, of an offence listed in Sch.15B? — YES → The court may deal with the offender by imposing whichever of the following measures is appropriate: A community order; A commensurate determinate sentence; An extended sentence of imprisonment (the custodial term may be of any length, at least twelve months)

NO (from "Is the offence punishable with life imprisonment?") →

↓ NO

Would the offence justify a determinate sentence of at least four years? — YES → The court may deal with the offender by imposing whichever of the following measures is appropriate: A community order; A commensurate determinate sentence; An extended sentence of imprisonment (the custodial term must be at least four years)

↓ NO

The court should pass an appropriate commensurate determinate sentence or community order

Sentencing Referencer

Dangerous Offenders—Young Offenders

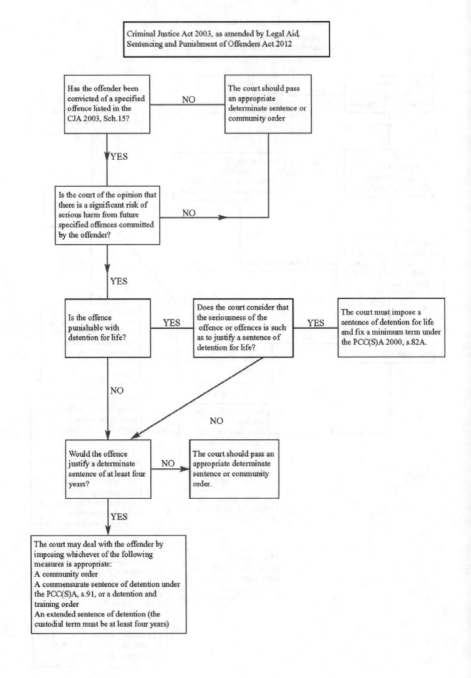

Criminal Justice Act 2003, as amended by Legal Aid, Sentencing and Punishment of Offenders Act 2012

Has the offender been convicted of a specified offence listed in the CJA 2003, Sch.15?

NO → The court should pass an appropriate determinate sentence or community order

↓ YES

Is the court of the opinion that there is a significant risk of serious harm from future specified offences committed by the offender?

NO →

↓ YES

Is the offence punishable with detention for life?

YES → Does the court consider that the seriousness of the offence or offences is such as to justify a sentence of detention for life?

YES → The court must impose a sentence of detention for life and fix a minimum term under the PCC(S)A 2000, s.82A.

NO ↓

NO

Would the offence justify a determinate sentence of at least four years?

NO → The court should pass an appropriate determinate sentence or community order.

↓ YES

The court may deal with the offender by imposing whichever of the following measures is appropriate:
A community order
A commensurate sentence of detention under the PCC(S)A, s.91, or a detention and training order
An extended sentence of detention (the custodial term must be at least four years)

Disqualification from Driving

Begin by identifying the category to which the offence with which you are concerned belongs, and then follow the instructions. Repeat the process for each offence, but bear in mind the restrictions on imposing penalty points for offences committed on the same occasion and on imposing more than one disqualification in penalty point cases.

All disqualifications run concurrently.

OFFENCES SUBJECT TO OBLIGATORY DISQUALIFICATION:

Causing death by dangerous driving	3–11
Causing serious injury by dangerous driving	3–11
Dangerous driving	3–11
Causing death by careless driving while under the influence of drink or drugs	3–11
Driving or attempting to drive while unfit	3–11
Driving or attempting to drive with excess alcohol	3–11
Failing to provide a specimen for analysis (driving or attempting to drive)	3–11
Racing or speed trials	3–11
Manslaughter	3–11
Aggravated vehicle taking	3–11

GO TO "OBLIGATORY DISQUALIFICATION"

OFFENCES SUBJECT TO DISCRETIONARY DISQUALIFICATION BUT NOT ENDORSEMENT:

Stealing or attempting to steal a motor vehicle

Taking a motor vehicle without consent, or being carried

Going equipped to steal a motor vehicle

GO TO DISCRETIONARY DISQUALIFICATION

OFFENCES SUBJECT TO OBLIGATORY ENDORSEMENT (SELECTED; FOR OTHER OFFENCES SEE ROAD TRAFFIC OFFENDERS ACT 1988, SCH.2):

Careless driving	3–9
Being in charge of a vehicle when unfit to drive	10
Being in charge of a vehicle with excess alcohol level	10
Failing to provide a breath specimen	4
Failing to provide a specimen when disqualification not obligatory	10
Leaving vehicle in dangerous position	3
Failing to comply with directions or signs	3
Using vehicle in dangerous condition	3
Driving without licence	3–6
Driving with uncorrected eyesight	3
Driving while disqualified	6
Using vehicle without insurance	6–8
Failing to stop after accident	5–10
Failing to give information as to driver	3

GO TO "PENALTY POINTS"

Note: An offender convicted of any offence may be disqualified from driving under the P.C.C.(S.)A. s.147.

All references are to the Road Traffic Offenders Act 1988 as amended by the Road Traffic Act. 1991.

Obligatory Disqualification

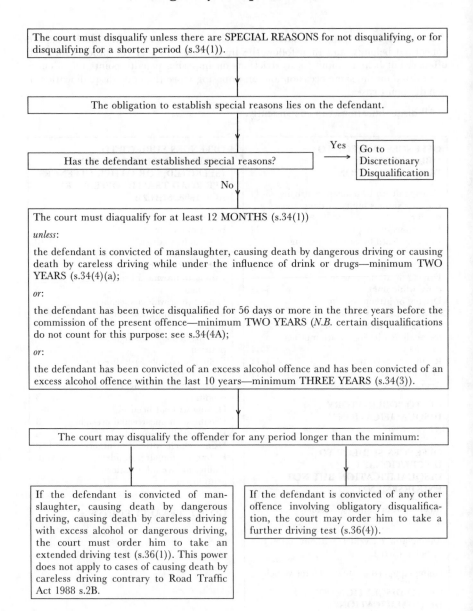

The court must disqualify unless there are SPECIAL REASONS for not disqualifying, or for disqualifying for a shorter period (s.34(1)).

The obligation to establish special reasons lies on the defendant.

Has the defendant established special reasons?

Yes → Go to Discretionary Disqualification

No

The court must diaqualify for at least 12 MONTHS (s.34(1))

unless:

the defendant is convicted of manslaughter, causing death by dangerous driving or causing death by careless driving while under the influence of drink or drugs—minimum TWO YEARS (s.34(4)(a);

or:

the defendant has been twice disqualified for 56 days or more in the three years before the commission of the present offence—minimum TWO YEARS (*N.B.* certain disqualifications do not count for this purpose: see s.34(4A);

or:

the defendant has been convicted of an excess alcohol offence and has been convicted of an excess alcohol offence within the last 10 years—minimum THREE YEARS (s.34(3)).

The court may disqualify the offender for any period longer than the minimum:

If the defendant is convicted of manslaughter, causing death by dangerous driving, causing death by careless driving with excess alcohol or dangerous driving, the court must order him to take an extended driving test (s.36(1)). This power does not apply to cases of causing death by careless driving contrary to Road Traffic Act 1988 s.2B.

If the defendant is convicted of any other offence involving obligatory disqualification, the court may order him to take a further driving test (s.36(4)).

Penalty Points

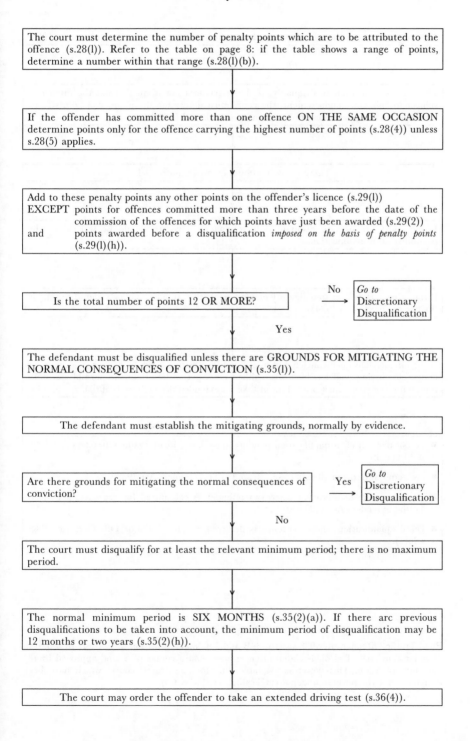

The court must determine the number of penalty points which are to be attributed to the offence (s.28(l)). Refer to the table on page 8: if the table shows a range of points, determine a number within that range (s.28(l)(b)).

If the offender has committed more than one offence ON THE SAME OCCASION determine points only for the offence carrying the highest number of points (s.28(4)) unless s.28(5) applies.

Add to these penalty points any other points on the offender's licence (s.29(l))
EXCEPT points for offences committed more than three years before the date of the commission of the offences for which points have just been awarded (s.29(2))
and points awarded before a disqualification *imposed on the basis of penalty points* (s.29(l)(h)).

Is the total number of points 12 OR MORE? — No → Go to Discretionary Disqualification

Yes

The defendant must be disqualified unless there are GROUNDS FOR MITIGATING THE NORMAL CONSEQUENCES OF CONVICTION (s.35(l)).

The defendant must establish the mitigating grounds, normally by evidence.

Are there grounds for mitigating the normal consequences of conviction? — Yes → Go to Discretionary Disqualification

No

The court must disqualify for at least the relevant minimum period; there is no maximum period.

The normal minimum period is SIX MONTHS (s.35(2)(a)). If there arc previous disqualifications to be taken into account, the minimum period of disqualification may be 12 months or two years (s.35(2)(h)).

The court may order the offender to take an extended driving test (s.36(4)).

Discretionary Disqualification

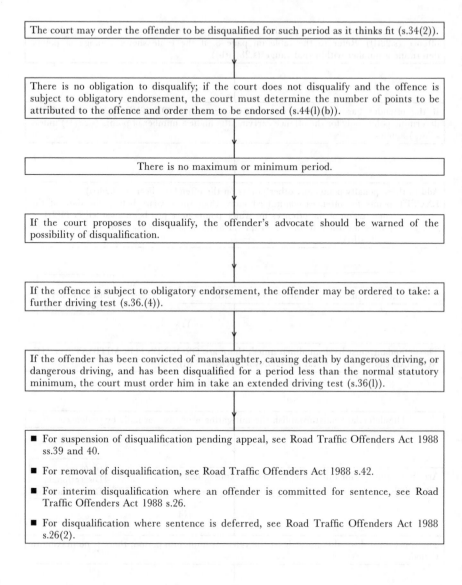

The court may order the offender to be disqualified for such period as it thinks fit (s.34(2)).

There is no obligation to disqualify; if the court does not disqualify and the offence is subject to obligatory endorsement, the court must determine the number of points to be attributed to the offence and order them to be endorsed (s.44(1)(b)).

There is no maximum or minimum period.

If the court proposes to disqualify, the offender's advocate should be warned of the possibility of disqualification.

If the offence is subject to obligatory endorsement, the offender may be ordered to take: a further driving test (s.36.(4)).

If the offender has been convicted of manslaughter, causing death by dangerous driving, or dangerous driving, and has been disqualified for a period less than the normal statutory minimum, the court must order him in take an extended driving test (s.36(1)).

- For suspension of disqualification pending appeal, see Road Traffic Offenders Act 1988 ss.39 and 40.

- For removal of disqualification, see Road Traffic Offenders Act 1988 s.42.

- For interim disqualification where an offender is committed for sentence, see Road Traffic Offenders Act 1988 s.26.

- For disqualification where sentence is deferred, see Road Traffic Offenders Act 1988 s.26(2).

Road Traffic Offenders Act 988 ss.34A, 34B and 34C make provision for a court to order an offender convicted of alcohol-related offences to attend a course of a kind approved by the Secretary of State. This power is available only to magistrates' courts which have been designated for the purpose under Road Traffic Act 1991 s.3(3).

Sentences for Young Offenders

Age on date of conviction:	10	11	12	13	14	15	16	17	18	19	20
Custodial sentences:											
Detention s.91	1	1	1	1	1	1	1	1	N	N	N
Detention and training order	N	N	2	2	2	Y	Y	Y	N	N	N
Detention in a young offender institution	N	N	N	N	N	N	N	N	Y	Y	Y
Extended sentence of detention	3	3	3	3	3	3	3	3	N	N	N
Extended sentence of detention in a young offender institution	N	N	N	N	N	N	N	N	3	3	3

Y = the order is available
N = the order is not available
1, 2 or 3 = refer to footnote

1 If convicted on indictment of an offence to which the P.C.C.(S.)A. 2000 s.91 applies.

2 If a "persistent offender".

3 If convicted of a specified offence and the court considers that there is a significant risk of serious harm.

Community Sentences—Young Offenders

Age on date of conviction:	10	11	12	13	14	15	16	17	18	19	20
Action plan order	3	3	3	3	3	3	3	3	N	N	N
Attendance centre Order	3	3	3	3	3	3	3	3	1	1	1
Community order (Criminal Justice Act 2003)	N	N	N	N	N	N	N	N	2	2	2
Community punishment Order	N	N	N	N	N	N	3	3	1	1	1
Community rehabilitation Order	N	N	N	N	N	N	3	3	1	1	1
Community punishment and Rehabilitation order	N	N	N	N	N	N	3	3	1	1	1
Curfew order	3	3	3	3	3	3	3	3	1	1	1
Drug treatment and testing order	N	N	N	N	N	N	3	3	1	1	1
Exclusion order	6	6	6	6	6	6	6	6	7	7	7
Referral order	4	4	4	4	4	4	4	4	N	N	N
Reparation order	5	5	5	5	5	5	5	5	N	N	N
Supervision order	3	3	3	3	3	3	3	3	N	N	N
Youth rehabilitation order	8	8	8	8	8	8	8	8	N	N	N

Y = the order is available
N = the order is not available
1, 2, 3, 4, 5, 6, 7, 8 = refer to footnote

1 If the offence was committed before April 4, 2005.

2 If the offence was committed on or after April 4, 2005.

3 If the offence was committed before November 30, 2009.

4 Mandatory if compulsory referral conditions apply.

5 If the court has been notified that arrangements are available.

6 If the offence was committed before November 30, 2009, and the court has been notified that arrangements are available.

7 If the offence was committed before April 4, 2005, and the court has been notified that arrangements are available

8 If the offence was committed on or after November 30, 2009.

Note: discharges are available in all cases.

Criminal Justice Act 2003 Sch.15

The following offences are "specified offences" for the purposes of s.224 of the Act.

SPECIFIED VIOLENT OFFENCES

Manslaughter.

Kidnapping.

False imprisonment.

Offences under any of the following provisions of the **Offences against the Person Act 1861:**

ss.4, 16, **18, 20,** 21 , 22 , 23, 27 , 28, 29, 30, 31, 32, 35, 37 , 38, **47.**

Explosive Substances Act 1883 ss.2, 3.

Infant Life (Preservation) Act 1929 s.1.

Children and Young Persons Act 1933 s.1.

Infanticide Act 1938, s.1.

Offences under any of the of the following provisions of the **Firearms Act 1968:** ss.16, 16A 17(1) or 17(2), 18.

Offences under any of the following provisions of the **Theft Act 1968: s.8,** 9 (burglary with intent to inflict grievous bodily harm on a person, or do unlawful damage to a building or anything in it, not burglary with intent to steal) 10, 12A, (aggravated vehicle-taking involving an accident which caused the death of any person).

Offences under any of the following provisions of the **Criminal Damage Act 1971**: ss.1, 1(2), (destroying or damaging property other than an offence of arson).

Taking of Hostages Act 1982 s.1.

Offences under any of the following provisions of the **Aviation Security Act 1982**: ss.1, 2, 3, 4.

Mental Health Act 1983 s.127.

Prohibition of Female Circumcision Act 1985 s.1.

Offences under any of the following provisions of the **Public Order Act 1986**: ss.1, 2, 3.

Criminal Justice Act 1988 s.134.

Road Traffic Act 1988 s.1, 3A.

Aviation and Maritime Security Act 1990 s. 1, 9, 10, 11, 12, 13.

Channel Tunnel (Security) Order 1994 Pt II.

Protection from Harassment Act 1997 s.4, 4A.

Crime and Disorder Act 1998, ss.29, 31(1)(a) or (b).

Offences committed on or after January 12, 2010 under any of the following provisions of the **Terrorism Act 2000**: ss.54, 56, 57, 59.

International Criminal Court Act 2001 ss.51, 52.

Offences *committed on or after January 12 2010* under any of following the provisions of the   Anti-terrorism, Crime and Security Act 2001: ss.47, 50, 113

Female Genital Mutilation Act 2003 ss. 1, 2, 3.

Domestic Violence, Crime and Victims Act 2004 s.5.

Offences *committed on or after January 12, 2010* under any of following the provisions of the **Terrorism Act 2006**: ss.5, 6, 9, 10, 11.

Aiding, abetting, counselling, procuring or inciting the commission of a specified violent offence, conspiring or attempting to commit a specified violent offence.

Attempted murder or conspiring to commit murder.

An offence under the Serious Crime Act 2007 committed with reference to a specified violent offence.

SPECIFIED SEXUAL OFFENCES

Note: the offences set out in italics were repealed on May 1, 2004, and cannot be committed after April 4, 2005.

*Offences under any of the following provisions of the **Sexual Offences Act 1956**: ss.1, 2, 3, 4, 5, 6, 7, 9, 10, 11, 14, 15 16, 17, 19, 20, 21,22,23,24,25, 26, 27, 28, 29, 32, 33.*

Mental Health Act 1959 s.128.

Indecency with Children Act 1960 s.1.

Sexual Offences Act 1967 s.4, 5.

Criminal Law Act 1977 s.54.

Protection of Children Act 1978 s.1.

Customs and Excise Management Act 1979 s.170, in relation to goods prohibited to be imported under s.42 of the Customs Consolidation Act 1876 (c.36) (indecent or obscene articles).

Criminal Justice Act 1988 s.160.

Sexual Offences Act 2003.

All offences contrary to the Sexual Offences Act 2003 are specified offences, with the exception of s.51A (soliciting), s.53A (paying for sexual services of a prostitute subjected to force etc.) and s.71 (sexual activity in public lavatory).

Aiding, abetting, counselling, procuring or inciting the commission of a specified sexual offence, conspiring or attempting to commit a specified sexual offence.

An offence under the Serious Crime Act 2007 committed with reference to a specified sexual offence.

Criminal Justice Act 2003 Sch.15B

The following offences are listed in **Part 1** of Schedule 15B *(offences for which a life sentence must be imposed)*:

1. Manslaughter.

2. An offence under section 4 of the Offences against the Person Act 1861 (soliciting murder).

3. An offence under section 18 of that Act (wounding with intent to cause grievous bodily harm).

4. An offence under section 16 of the Firearms Act 1968 (possession of a firearm with intent to endanger life).

5. An offence under section 17(1) of that Act (use of a firearm to resist arrest).

6. An offence under section 18 of that Act (carrying a firearm with criminal intent).

7. An offence of robbery under section 8 of the Theft Act 1968 where, at some time during the commission of the offence, the offender had in his possession a firearm or an imitation firearm within the meaning of the Firearms Act 1968.

   Where the question arises whether a robbery committed was an "offence of robbery under section 8 of the Theft Act 1968 where, at some time during the commission of the offence, the offender had in his possession a firearm or an imitation firearm within the meaning of the Firearms Act 1968", it must be established or admitted that the offender was a party to the robbery which to his knowledge involved the possession of a firearm or imitation firearm by one or more of those involved in robbery.

8. An offence under section 1 of the Protection of Children Act 1978 (indecent images of children).

9. An offence under section 56 of the Terrorism Act 2000 (directing terrorist organisation).

10. An offence under section 57 of that Act (possession of article for terrorist purposes).

11. An offence under section 59 of that Act (inciting terrorism overseas) if the offender is liable on conviction on indictment to imprisonment for life.

12. An offence under section 47 of the Anti-terrorism, Crime and Security Act 2001 (use etc. of nuclear weapons).

13. An offence under section 50 of that Act (assisting or inducing certain weapons-related acts overseas).

14. An offence under section 113 of that Act (use of noxious substance or thing to cause harm or intimidate).

15. An offence under section 1 of the Sexual Offences Act 2003 (rape).

16. An offence under section 2 of that Act (assault by penetration).

17. An offence under section 4 of that Act (causing a person to engage in sexual activity without consent) if the offender is liable on conviction on indictment to imprisonment for life.

18. An offence under section 5 of that Act (rape of a child under 13).

19. An offence under section 6 of that Act (assault of a child under 13 by penetration).

20. An offence under section 7 of that Act (sexual assault of a child under 13).

21. An offence under section 8 of that Act (causing or inciting a child under 13 to engage in sexual activity).

22. An offence under section 9 of that Act (sexual activity with a child).

23. An offence under section 10 of that Act (causing or inciting a child to engage in sexual activity).

24. An offence under section 11 of that Act (engaging in sexual activity in the presence of a child).

25. An offence under section 12 of that Act (causing a child to watch a sexual act).

26. An offence under section 14 of that Act (arranging or facilitating commission of a child sex offence).

27. An offence under section 15 of that Act (meeting a child following sexual grooming etc.).

28. An offence under section 25 of that Act (sexual activity with a child family member) if the offender is aged 18 or over at the time of the offence.

29. An offence under section 26 of that Act (inciting a child family member to engage in sexual activity) if the offender is aged 18 or over at the time of the offence.

30. An offence under section 30 of that Act (sexual activity with a person with a mental disorder impeding choice) if the offender is liable on conviction on indictment to imprisonment for life.

31. An offence under section 31 of that Act (causing or inciting a person with a mental disorder to engage in sexual activity) if the offender is liable on conviction on indictment to imprisonment for life.

32. An offence under section 34 of that Act (inducement, threat or deception to procure sexual activity with a person with a mental disorder) if the offender is liable on conviction on indictment to imprisonment for life.

33. An offence under section 35 of that Act (causing a person with a mental disorder to engage in or agree to engage in sexual activity by inducement etc.) if the offender is liable on conviction on indictment to imprisonment for life.

34. An offence under section 47 of that Act (paying for sexual services of a child) against a person aged under 16.

35. An offence under section 48 of that Act (causing or inciting child prostitution or pornography).

36. An offence under section 49 of that Act (controlling a child prostitute or a child involved in pornography).

37. An offence under section 50 of that Act (arranging or facilitating child prostitution or pornography).

38. An offence under section 62 of that Act (committing an offence with intent to commit a sexual offence) if the offender is liable on conviction on indictment to imprisonment for life.

39. An offence under section 5 of the Domestic Violence, Crime and Victims Act 2004 (causing or allowing the death of a child or vulnerable adult).

40. An offence under section 5 of the Terrorism Act 2006 (preparation of terrorist acts).

41. An offence under section 9 of that Act (making or possession of radioactive device or materials).

42. An offence under section 10 of that Act (misuse of radioactive devices or material and misuse and damage of facilities).

43. An offence under section 11 of that Act (terrorist threats relating to radioactive devices, materials or facilities).

44. (1) An attempt to commit an offence specified in the preceding paragraphs of this Part of this Schedule ("a listed offence") or murder.

    (2) Conspiracy to commit a listed offence or murder.

    (3) Incitement to commit a listed offence or murder.

(4) An offence under Part 2 of the Serious Crime Act 2007 in relation to which a listed offence or murder is the offence (or one of the offences) which the person intended or believed would be committed.

(5) Aiding, abetting, counselling or procuring the commission of a listed offence.

The following offences are listed in Parts 2, 3 and 4 of Schedule 15B *(offences which may amount to a previous offence)*:

45. Murder.

46. Any offence that—

   (a) was abolished (with or without savings) before the coming into force of this Schedule, and

   (b) would, if committed on the day on which the offender was convicted of that offence have constituted an offence specified in Part 1 of this Schedule.

47. An offence under section 70 of the Army Act 1955, section 70 of the Air Force Act 1955 or section 42 of the Naval Discipline Act 1957 as respects which the corresponding civil offence (within the meaning of the Act in question) is an offence specified in Part 1 or 2 of this Schedule.

48. An offence under section 42 of the Armed Forces Act 2006 as respects which the corresponding offence under the law of England and Wales (within the meaning given by that section) is an offence specified in Part 1 or 2 of this Schedule.

49. An offence for which the person was convicted in Scotland, Northern Ireland or a member State other than the United Kingdom and which, if committed in England and Wales at the time of the conviction, would have constituted an offence specified in Part 1 or 2 of this Schedule.

Counter-Terrorism Act 2008 Sch.2

The following offences are listed in Sch.2 to the Act:

Common law offences: murder, manslaughter, kidnapping, abduction.

Statutory offences: offences against

Anti-Terrorism Crime and Security Act 2001 ss.47 and 114;

Aviation and Maritime Security Act ss.1, 9, 10, 11, 14(4) (in relation to an offence under s.9 or 11 of the Act);

Aviation Security Act 1982 ss.1, 2, 3, 4, 6(2);

Biological Weapons Act 1974 s.1;

Chemical Weapons Act 1996 ss.2, 11;

Explosive Substances Act 1883 ss.2, 3, 4, 5;

Nuclear Material (Offences) Act 1983 ss.1B, 1C, 2;

Offences against the Person Act 1861 ss.4, 23, 28 , 29, 30, 64.

Taking of Hostages Act 1982 s.1.

The Channel Tunnel (Security) Order 1994, Pt 2.

Any ancillary offence in relation to an offence specified in the Schedule.